Urban transformation and urban governance

Shaping the competitive city of the future

Edited by Martin Boddy

First published in Great Britain in October 2003 by

The Policy Press
University of Bristol
Fourth Floor, Beacon House
Queen's Road
Bristol BS8 1QU
UK

Tel no +44 (0)117 331 4054
Fax no +44 (0)117 331 4093
E-mail tpp-info@bristol.ac.uk
www.policypress.org.uk

Reprinted 2004

Transferred to Digital Print 2006

ISBN-10 1 86134 529 1
ISBN-13 978 1 86134 529 5

Martin Boddy is Associate Dean and Professor of Urban and Regional Studies in the Faculty of the Built Environment, University of the West of England, Bristol.

Cover design by Qube Design Associates, Bristol
Cover photograph supplied by kind permission of www.bristol-city.gov.uk
Printed in Great Britain by Marston Book Services, Oxford

Contents

List of figures and tables

Figures

Tables

Preface

This is one of a series of published reports of the 'Cities, Competitiveness and Cohesion' research programme funded by the Economic and Social Research Council (ESRC) (grant number L130251006), with additional support from the Department of the Environment, Transport and the Regions. This £4 million programme included 23 different projects and ran from 1997 to 2002 (see Boddy and Parkinson, 2004: forthcoming, for an account of programme findings as a whole). This volume presents analysis and findings from one of four 'integrative city studies' included in the programme.

The study was carried out by a joint team from the University of the West of England (UWE) and the University of Bristol, directed by Martin Boddy. The team at the time included Keith Bassett, Martin Boddy, Shaun French, Andrew Leyshon and Nigel Thrift at the University of Bristol and Ron Griffiths, Christine Lambert, Ian Smith and Murray Stewart at UWE. Nick Oatley and Nigel Taylor at UWE also contributed to the early stages of the project. The chapters in this volume have been individually authored as indicated. The work presented here, however, very much draws on the work of the team as a whole and on extensive discussion and debate throughout the course of the project. Outputs from the project as a whole are listed on the ESRC's *Regard* website (www.regard.ac.uk) and can be consulted by entering the ESRC reference number given above.

The study drew extensively on interviews and discussion with a wide range of representatives of business, community and voluntary sector organisations and public sector bodies locally. We would like to acknowledge the major importance of this input to the study and to thank them for this. We also benefited greatly from extensive discussion with members of the other project teams in the overall programme, including members of the other integrative city studies, especially Ivan Turok and colleagues in Glasgow and Edinburgh, Alan Harding and colleagues in Manchester and Liverpool and Ian Gordon and colleagues in London. We would also like to thank the programme's three directors, Duncan Maclennan, Ade Kearns in the early stages, and particularly Michael Parkinson, for their invaluable guidance and support.

Martin Boddy
September 2003

Notes on contributors

Correct at time of first printing.

Keith Bassett is Senior Lecturer in Geography in the School of Geographical Sciences, University of Bristol.

Martin Boddy is Professor of Urban and Regional Studies and Associate Dean (Research and Consultancy) in the Faculty of the Built Environment, University of the West of England (UWE), Bristol.

Shaun French is Lecturer in Geography in the School of Geography, University of Nottingham.

Ron Griffiths is Principal Lecturer in Urban Planning in the Faculty of the Built Environment, UWE, Bristol.

Andrew Leyshon is Professor of Economic and Social Geography in the School of Geography, University of Nottingham.

Christine Lambert is Reader in Urban Planning in the Faculty of the Built Environment, UWE, Bristol.

Ian Smith is Senior Research Fellow in the Faculty of the Built Environment, UWE, Bristol.

Murray Stewart is an independent consultant and Visiting Professor in the Faculty of the Built Environment, UWE, Bristol.

Introduction

Martin Boddy

Cities and urban change are now central to both academic and policy agendas at national, European and wider international scales. Urban regeneration, sustainable development, social exclusion and social cohesion, managing the pressures of urban growth, and the role of cities and urban assets in securing economic competitiveness – together present major challenges for policy makers, practitioners, policy analysts and academic researchers alike.

In policy terms in particular, towns and cities are increasingly taking centre stage. In the case of the UK, Lord Rogers' Urban Taskforce report (Urban Task Force, 1999) offered a new vision for urban regeneration and renaissance. The UK government's Urban White Paper (DETR, 2000a) then set out its future agenda for urban policy and urban development. The government's Social Exclusion Unit also produced its wide-ranging *National strategy for neighbourhood renewal* to tackle the problems of poor neighbourhoods (SEU, 1998, 2001a). And most recently, the government has set out its action plan for sustainable communities – the national Communities Plan, which includes plans for major new and expanded settlements together with action on housing affordability and quality of provision (ODPM, 2003a). Urban areas in the UK continue to exhibit persistent concentrations of poverty and social exclusion with economic restructuring and demographic shifts reflected in increasing social and spatial polarisation. Meanwhile the debate continues over the massive projected increase in household numbers, the obstacles to increased brownfield development and the threat to more rural areas of creeping urbanisation, as well as the challenge this poses for environmental issues and sustainability.

Cities are also seen increasingly as key nodes in terms of economic development, competitiveness and innovation, particularly in the context of increasing globalisation and mobility of people, information, finance and investment. The government has been working with the eight English 'core cities', the largest city-regions outside of London, to look at how their contribution to economic competitiveness can be enhanced (CCG, 2003). Thus, cities are of increasing importance in terms of economic competitiveness at regional, national and international scales. Cities are seen as critically important to the development of the knowledge-based new economy. And the attractiveness of cities and city living are critical factors that affect their capacity to attract and retain key knowledge workers and the creative classes. Urban renaissance and downtown redevelopment, as well as the perceived green shoots of urban turnaround, are thus eagerly sought after. At the same time, there is increasing concern that the traditional framework of containment and planning constraint might inhibit business investment in those parts of the country that give it competitive strength. Consequently, UK competitiveness may be damaged.

This volume draws on the major programme of urban research funded by the UK Economic and Social Research Council (ESRC) under its 'Cities, Competitiveness and Cohesion' research programme, supported by the government's then Department for Transport, Local Government and the Regions (DTLR). The work presented here addresses major issues in current urban debate and policy discourse, including:

- the dynamics of employment and population change and long-term decentralisation, and de-urbanisation;
- the challenges posed by household growth, the resulting development pressures and the brownfield/greenfield development debate;
- more recent signs of urban turnaround and urban renaissance;
- social exclusion, social cohesion and social polarisation which persist even in the face of competitive success;
- the role of knowledge-based new economy sectors, including the rapidly changing financial services and the more recently prominent cultural and media sectors;
- new urban forms, the growth of edge-city development peripheral to and potentially challenging the role of the traditional 'centred city';
- the changing spatial architecture of urban and regional governance and its potential role in securing competitive advantage, social cohesion and neighbourhood renewal.

These themes are addressed by combining a far-reaching case study of the Bristol city-region together with a wide range of data and information both from other studies in the 'Cities, Competitiveness and Cohesion' research programme and from other national and international sources. The Bristol city-region study was one of four, large-scale 'integrative city studies' undertaken within the overall ESRC programme. Other city studies focused on London, Edinburgh and Glasgow, and Liverpool and Manchester. The aim of these four studies was to address in an integrated fashion the three interlocking programme themes of competitiveness, cohesion and governance. In the context of the overall programme, Bristol exemplified a large, free-standing, economically buoyant city-region in southern England, albeit marked by significant and persistent spatially concentrated exclusion and deprivation.

The project drew on a wide range of methodologies, generated a substantial body of original data (both quantitative and qualitative) and made extensive use of secondary sources. Key information sources included: questionnaire surveys of local businesses; face-to-face interviews with major employers, policy professionals and politicians, private sector property

professionals and representatives of community and voluntary sector bodies; and extensive use of secondary data sources including Neighbourhood Statistics, the 2001 Census, and other data sets available from National Statistics and NOMIS.

The case study itself focuses largely on what we term the 'Bristol city-region'. We use the term to signify the broadly defined functional urban area of Bristol rather than the more tightly drawn administrative City of Bristol defined by the local authority boundary (see Figure 1.1). Pragmatically, the city-region can be defined in terms of the Bristol travel-to-work area. We also focus for practical purposes on the City of Bristol, together with the three adjoining local authority areas of South Gloucestershire, Bath and North East Somerset, and North Somerset.

The chapters of this volume each combine broadly framed discussion together with case-study material. Chapter 2 sets out the major dimensions of change impacting on Britain's towns and cities. It goes on to look in more detail at how these have impacted in the Bristol city-region and some of the implications of these changes. As well as setting the context for the chapters that follow, it also represents a contribution to our more general understanding of the dynamics of urban change. Chapter 3 then focuses on the changing spatial structure and form of urban areas and the forces driving this spatial transformation. It describes the emergence of edge-of-city developments exemplified by major growth on Bristol's north fringe, the role of policy and governance in these processes of change and their wider implications for the future of the city-region.

Central to the competitive success of cities over recent years has been their capacity to capture investment and employment growth in the new 'knowledge economy'. Key elements of this 'new' economy have been financial and business services and the cultural and media sectors. Chapter 4, therefore, focuses on the urban impacts of the financial services sector in Bristol and other major financial centres in the UK. Bristol benefited early on from the growth of financial services. More recently, the sector has been transformed by large-scale restructuring with wide-ranging implications for the spatial logic of the sector that the chapter goes on to explore. It also looks at the links between

Figure 1.1: Bristol city-region

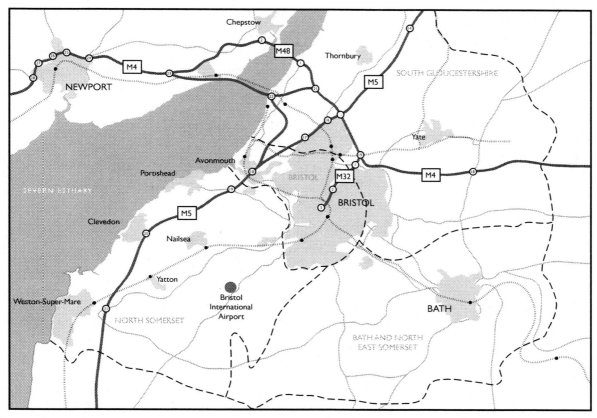

Source: Graphics Unit, UWE, Bristol

financial services and social exclusion and the implications for policy agendas.

Chapter 5 turns to the culture and media sector and the 'creative' activities, which have increasingly been seen as central to both competitive success and quality of life. Cities have increasingly sought to harness culture, media and creative activities for the purpose of economic and social regeneration. This chapter looks at the role of the culture and media sectors in the Bristol city-region, the emergence of a 'cultural strategy' in the city, the extent to which cultural industries constitute a localised cluster of activities, and the role of cultural activities in terms of urban regeneration and social inclusion.

Chapter 6 focuses directly on the key issues of social exclusion and social cohesion. It summarises the contemporary debate and then documents the persistent concentration of social exclusion and deprivation evident in the context of what is, more generally, a prosperous and demonstrably competitive city-region. It points in particular to the striking

scale of educational deprivation and underperformance in parts of the city-region, including both the core inner city and outer social housing estates as a significant driver of exclusion and polarisation.

In recent years, UK urban policy has been characterised by constant change and the proliferation of policy instruments and institutional structures. New forms of urban governance based on multiple stakeholders and the central importance of collaborative capacity are increasingly to the fore. Chapter 7 discusses the nature of new urban governance and urban policy based on the evolving structures of governance in the Bristol city-region and the dilemmas that this throws up. Finally, Chapter 8 brings together key findings and draws out the more general implications. It focuses in particular on the links between competitiveness, cohesion and urban governance and the lessons to be drawn on the capacity for shaping the urban future.

2

The changing city

Martin Boddy

For much of the postwar period, British cities have seen distinctive shifts in the location of population and employment: from core urban areas to the suburbs and from the conurbations and large cities in favour of smaller towns and cities and more rural areas. Combined with this has been a persistent north/south divide in terms of population and employment trends. These underlying trends form a backdrop to the shifts in population, households and employment in different towns and cities across the whole of Britain.

Employment change

In terms of employment, the conurbations, larger free-standing cities across the country as a whole and smaller northern cities all saw their total share of national employment fall in the period 1959-97. Smaller southern cities, on the other hand, increased their overall share of employment (see Table 2.1). The planned new and expanded towns succeeded in generating particularly rapid employment growth.

Employment change can be seen as a key indicator of the overall competitive strength of particular types of urban area. Employment growth and the attraction of new businesses and investment are indicative of the attractiveness of particular places and the particular bundle of assets they offer for business activity.

Shifts in employment in part reflect structural changes in the nature of economic activity and industrial structure. Those places best able to attract businesses and investment in expanding sectors, such as financial and business services and advanced manufacturing, have clearly done well. Other places have suffered in particular from their legacy of employment in older manufacturing: coal, steel, textiles and shipbuilding especially. It is this that underlies the north/south divide. It is a legacy that lingers on in the contrasting economic fortune of northern and southern cities, contrasts in terms of unemployment and economic inactivity and the 'jobs gap' between north and south.

Table 2.1: Employment change by type of urban area (1959-97)

	Employment, including self-employment (000s)					Change (%)			Share (% of GB total)	
	1959	1971	1981	1991	1997	1959 -81	1981 -91	1991 -97	Share in 1959	Share in 1997
Conurbations	10,074	9,351	8,688	8,395	8,710	−13.8	−3.4	3.8	43.7	33.8
Free-standing	33,694	3,496	3,484	3,580	3,647	3.4	2.7	1.9	14.6	14.1
'Northern'	11,054	1,104	1,084	1,097	1,107	−2.0	1.2	0.9	4.8	4.3
'Southern'	17,524	2,010	2,129	2,384	2,529	21.5	12.0	6.1	7.6	9.8
Expanded	5,194	594	651	706	766	25.5	8.5	8.5	2.3	3.0
New Towns	4,484	552	649	808	918	44.8	24.5	13.7	1.9	3.6
Coastal	3,944	412	421	464	457	6.8	10.3	−1.5	1.7	1.8
Britain	230,344	23,476	23,298	24,647	25,775	1.1	5.8	4.6	100.0	100.0

Urban exodus

It is a broadly similar pattern in terms of population. The country's major conurbations in particular saw their share of total population fall back significantly in the period 1951-91 (Table 2.2). So too, to a lesser extent, have the larger free-standing cities and the smaller northern cities. On the other hand, smaller cities in the south, together with the new and expanded towns, saw considerable expansion in their share of total population.

Across the country as a whole, however, the net effect in terms of population movement has added up to what some observers have called an 'urban exodus'. From every level of the urban hierarchy, the net effect has been a cascade of population from urban cores areas to the suburbs and beyond, from larger to smaller urban areas, and from urban to more rural areas (Robson et al, 2000).

Shifts in population have reflected a combination of factors, both demographic and economic. 'Natural' growth in the population, the excess of births over deaths, varies by location. Patterns of net migration reflect to an extent underlying economic forces. Population tends to follow employment opportunities such that economically successful parts of the country with expanding employment opportunities tend also to attract population. Migration patterns including the net urban to rural shift also reflect residential preferences. The preferences of much of the British population for a less urban environment have been much discussed and are undoubtedly complex. However, larger urban areas do generally score less well on quality of life indicators, and perform less well in terms of education, crime, health and deprivation.

Net out-migration from the conurbations and larger urban areas has been selective in terms of skill level and occupational group. Rates of out-migration have generally been highest for professional, technical and managerial groups. Less-skilled, manual workers have been less likely to move. Consequently, the occupational and skill-base of the larger urban areas has shifted downwards. Again, this has reflected the shifting pattern of employment growth and job opportunities as well as the greater capacity of higher income groups to realise their preferences in terms of where they live.

The urban exodus from Greater London and the main conurbations continued in the 1990s with net out-migration to the rest of the UK averaging over 90,000 per annum over the period 1991-97. Add in the effects of international migration and natural population change, however, and the picture changes considerably. London was the major source of domestic net out-migration. Yet the scale of international in-migration to the capital more than outweighed this. Together with considerable natural growth, this meant that Greater London's population actually increased by over 200,000 in the period 1991-97. And while the other major conurbations had all suffered significant population loss in previous decades, there was a widespread turnaround in the 1990s. South Yorkshire, West Yorkshire and Greater Manchester all gained population. Merseyside, the West Midlands, Tyne and Wear and Clydeside lost population overall but at rates well below those of the two preceding decades. The larger free-standing cities and smaller northern cities that had also lost population in the 1980s again saw modest growth in the 1990s. Growth rates in smaller southern cities, and the expanded and new towns on the other hand slowed down to some extent.

Table 2.2: Population change by type of urban area (1951-97)

	Population			Changes (%)			Share (% of GB total)	
	1951	1991	1997 (est)	1951-81	1981-91	1991-97	1951	1997
Conurbations	19,320	17,096	17,328	−9.9	−1.7	1.4	39.4	30.9
Free-standing	6,866	6,944	7,040	2.1	−1.0	1.4	14.0	12.6
'Northern'	2,180	2,211	2,219	2.5	−1.1	0.3	4.5	4.0
'Southern'	3,410	4,709	4,823	33.0	3.8	2.4	7.0	8.6
Expanded	1,080	1,455	1,486	29.6	3.9	2.1	2.2	2.7
New Towns	576	1,253	1,293	97.5	10.1	3.2	1.2	2.3
Coastal	871	1,091	1,119	18.3	5.8	2.5	1.8	2.0
Britain	48,979	54,856	56,058	9.3	2.4	2.2	100.0	100.0

Household growth

There have been major shifts, then, in terms of both employment and population, which have impacted on urban areas. On top of this, the rate of increase in terms of household numbers has far-reaching implications for housing demand and housing provision both nationally and locally. Overall household numbers in England alone are projected to increase by four million between 1996 and 2021, an increase of 19%. Household numbers are increasing much more rapidly than population and are expected to increase by around 7% over the same period. Much of this increase in household numbers reflects growth in single-person households. It also reflects the increasing longevity of the population. Overall, this increase in household numbers is generating major demands for additional housing units across the country as a whole.

This has driven the government's overall strategy to secure a major increase in building on brownfield sites and to increase the density of development. It continues, however, to present major challenges to the planning system and to those planning authorities charged with meeting the government's targets. Even those conurbations that continue to lose population are seeing an expansion in numbers of households and increasing demand for new housing. Further down the urban hierarchy, and particularly in the more prosperous south, population growth and net in-migration combine with the expansion in household numbers to generate even greater pressures for new development.

The case of Bristol

A large free-standing city in prosperous 'southern England', the Bristol city-region as a whole has performed well in economic terms both in a regional context and compared with national and international benchmarks. Bristol City, at the geographical core, has a population of around 380,000 (2001) and total employment of some 230,000. Together with the three surrounding districts, Bath and North East Somerset, North Somerset, South Gloucestershire – a better approximation of the functional city-region in terms of economic links and commuting flows – the urban area includes a population of just under a million and

employment of 489,000[1]. Indicative of its competitive strength, the city-region has seen significant growth in both employment and population over recent years, and it has attracted net in-migration from the rest of the country. Reflecting this, rapid expansion of household numbers has generated major pressures in the housing market and has presented a severe challenge for the planning system in the face of pressures for new house building.

There are significant contrasts within the city-region as a whole in terms of economic performance and population change in recent years. Bristol City at the core of the city-region, has generally performed less well than the three surrounding districts. South Gloucestershire, formerly North Avon, has experienced particularly rapid expansion in terms of jobs and population. Here, 'edge-of-city' development just over the boundary with Bristol City on the 'North Fringe' of the urban area has been a major alternative focus for growth and investment to the core urban area.

Population change

In the period 1961-81, the Bristol city-region as a whole had a population growth rate close to the national average (Table 2.3). The 1980s and 1990s, however, saw population growth significantly ahead of national rates. As with other major urban areas in the UK, population decline in the urban core was juxtaposed with growth in the surrounding outer urban area. Thus, Bristol City itself at the core of the city-region, like many such areas nationally, suffered significant loss of population in the 1960s and 1970s: down by 12% in the period 1961-81. This slowed to just over 2% in the 1980s. The rate of population decline in the urban core then actually increased somewhat, rising to nearly 3% in the decade to 2001, based on Census of Population figures. In fact, this

[1] The official travel-to-work area as currently defined (usually taken as a working definition of a functional urban area) covers the four districts with the exception of the City of Bath and part of Bath and North East Somerset, and of Weston-super-Mare. The 2001 Census is likely to confirm the increasing functional integration across the former Bristol city-region as a whole. Therefore, the discussion here focuses on this area as a whole (referred to as the Bristol city-region).

ran counter to expectations based on mid-year population estimates produced prior to the Census of Population. These had suggested a more dramatic slowdown in population decline in core urban areas across the country as a whole, and in Bristol and Leeds, for example, a historic reversal from decline to modest growth. This led to what proved to be somewhat over-optimistic heralding of 'turn-around' or 'comeback cities'.

The outer part of the city-region, by contrast, had experienced spectacular growth in the 1960s and 1970s. Population growth in North Avon, now included within South Gloucestershire, was 69% in the period 1961-81; in Woodspring, now included in North Somerset, it was 48%. In the 1980s and 1990s, growth rates were more modest but, in South Gloucestershire and North Somerset in particular, still well ahead of national rates. South Gloucestershire continued to expand by over 10% in the decade up to the 2001 Census, compared with a decline of 2.9% in the City of Bristol. Thus, growth on Bristol's 'north fringe' over the period since the 1960s was comparable with average growth rates for new towns and expanded towns detailed above (Table 2.1).

Across the area as a whole, natural growth (excess of births over deaths) has contributed to population growth. The major factor, however, has been the level of net in-migration, reflecting economic expansion and job growth. In most years since 1984, the area has experienced positive net migration (in-flows exceed out-flows in all years apart from 1988-90).

Moreover, total flows of people in and out have been rising since 1990/91 (the low point for migration during the housing market recession); locally, the excess of inflow over outflow increased markedly up to 1988/89, falling back somewhat since then. This rate of sustained in-migration marks the Bristol city-region out from most other large urban areas.

Within the area as a whole, net in-migration and migration per head of population has been concentrated in particular on the outer parts of the city-region as a whole. There is also an important relationship with London and the South East region, out of which the Bristol area consistently gains population. Gains from other regions are also important, but more variable in line with the economic cycle.

On the other hand, there is a significant outflow of population from the city-region to the three adjoining counties. The city-region is typically a net importer of people aged 16-24, but loses population in older age groups[2]. A possible hypothesis, therefore, is that the Bristol area attracts large numbers of young people each year from the South East especially, but also other regions, and loses people at an older age, possibly at that point in the lifecycle

---

[2]   Data relate to the former county of Avon.

Table 2.3: Population change (1981-91, 1991-2001)

	1981	1991	2001
Bath and NE Somerset	161,491	163,135	169,163
Bristol City	401,194	392,174	380,753
North Somerset	162,864	179,213	188,827
South Gloucestershire	203,143	222,150	245,996
Bristol city-region	928,692	956,672	984,739
Britain	54,814500	55,831,363	57,148,695

	Change 1981-91		Change 1991-2001	
	abs.	%	abs.	%
Bath and NE Somerset	1,644	1.0	6,028	3.7
Bristol City	−9,020	−2.2	−11,421	−2.9
North Somerset	16,349	10.0	9,614	5.4
South Gloucestershire	19,007	9.4	23,846	10.7
Bristol city-region	27,980	3.0	28,067	2.9
Britain	1,016,863	1.9	1,317,332	2.4

Source: National Statistics, NOMIS, mid-year estimates, revised in line with 2001 Census

Figure 2.1: Net in-migration to Bristol city-region (1992-2001)

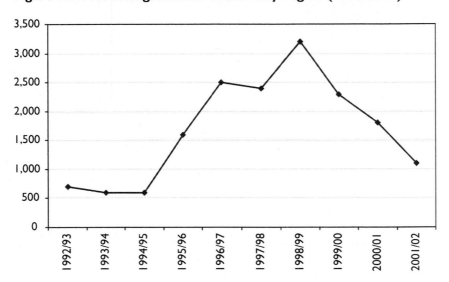

Source: NOMIS, National Health Service Central Register

when families are formed. This would be similar to the 'escalator' effect noted for London and the South East by Fielding (1991). In terms of the social make-up of migration, a snapshot is available from the 1991 Census based on analysis by Champion (1999). This suggests that migration movement is not in fact having any significant effect in terms of the socioeconomic profile of the city-region. This is unlike other urban areas, particularly in northern Britain, where significant net out-migration has depleted the remaining workforce of managerial, technical and professional workers.

Across the city-region as a whole, earlier decades saw a pattern of apparent decentralisation common to larger urban areas across the country as a whole, with population decline in the urban core combined with growth in surrounding areas. To some extent this reflected actual movement of people and households from the core to surrounding districts. To a greater extent, however, it reflected the scale of in-migration to the outer fringe of the city-region compared to movement into the urban core. It has been a case of differential growth rather than decentralisation pure and simple. Therefore, population change in the case of Bristol has not represented a simple process of counter-urbanisation or de-urbanisation; that is, a shift of population down the urban hierarchy. Rather, it has represented a process of localised decentralisation within essentially the same functional

city-region overlain by the differential impact of in-migration from beyond the city-region.

The gap in terms of population trends between core and periphery changed little in the 1990s compared with the previous decade. It may be that, most recently, the upsurge of new housing development in the core urban area coupled with the general decline in new greenfield housing development has been closing the gap to some extent. This is associated with specific developments including new house building and the regeneration of the former city docks. It may also reflect the increasing attractiveness of leisure provision and the urban environment in the urban core coupled with increasing problems of traffic congestion and inadequate public transport in surrounding areas. However, in the absence of hard evidence, this remains speculation.

Within Bristol City itself, population change has been somewhat uneven. Areas in the south in particular have seen population decline through the 1980s and 1990s, with little new house building and falling occupancy rates. Areas north and west of the centre have increased in population terms, with increasing intensity of use of the housing stock. The city centre itself has also grown in population, with development, as noted, in and around the former city docks and some conversion of offices to residential use.

Table 2.4: Household change (1981-91)

	1981	1991	Change 1981-91	Change 1981-91 (%)
Bristol city-region	333,806	379,466	45,660	13.7
Bath and NE Somerset	58,472	65,626	7,154	12.2
Bristol City	147,298	158,588	11,290	7.7
North Somerset	58,956	70,786	11,830	20.1
South Gloucestershire	69,080	84,466	15,386	22.3

Source: Census of Population, OPCS

Household growth

As is the case nationally, overall growth in households in the Bristol area has run well ahead of population change. Bristol represents an area where demographically driven household growth is overlaid on significant underlying growth in population. This had resulted in particularly strong pressures in terms of overall expansion in household numbers and resultant pressures in the housing market. Household growth across the area as a whole of nearly 14% (1981-91) was slightly ahead of national growth rates (Table 2.4). Rates of growth were considerably higher, however, in South Gloucestershire and North Somerset.

Again, as is the case nationally, growth in household numbers as a whole, reflects population trends, but with a general fall in household size overlaid. Average household size in the Bristol city-region is estimated at 2.32, slightly below the national averages. This probably reflects the higher proportion of single-person households locally compared to the national picture, along with growth in older, single-person households reflecting increased longevity, seen more generally.

As Table 2.4 illustrates, household growth is thus significantly higher than growth in population. While population in Bristol City fell slightly in the decade prior to 1991, the number of households actually increased by 8%. And population growth in North Somerset and South Gloucestershire of around 10%, rapid in itself by national standards, was far outpaced by growth in household numbers, running at 20+% in the decade leading up to 1991.

Estimates suggest that household growth across the Bristol city-region continued at about the same rate in the 1990s, increasing by an estimated 11.5% over the eight years between 1991 and 1999 (Table 2.5). Again, this was well ahead of population growth of 4.5% over the same period.

This has had major implications in terms of demand for housing, particularly in the outer areas, but also in the urban core where population growth itself has been much more modest. Growth generated by demographic processes is considerable even in circumstances where population growth is modest or absent. Estimates suggest that household growth continued to represent a major driver of housing demand in the 1990s over and above any continuing increase in the population itself. Trends in household structure would seem to suggest, moreover, that this is likely to be of continuing significance.

Students are an increasingly important section of the population in the area: important in terms of the dynamic of population growth. The city-region contains four universities, Bristol, Bath, Bath Spa and West of England, with some 40,000 students

Table 2.5: Estimated household change (1991-99)

	1991	1999	Change 1991-99	Change 1991-99 (%)
Bath and NE Somerset	65,626	71,000	5,374	8.2
Bristol City	158,588	174,000	15,412	9.7
North Somerset	70,786	79,000	8,214	11.6
South Gloucestershire	84,466	99,000	14,554	17.2
Bristol city-region	379,466	423,000	43,554	11.5

Source: Census of Population (1991), DTLR statistics on housing and households, estimated household numbers by local authority district (1999)

registered in 2001. It is estimated that by the end of the 1990s approaching 10% of Bristol City's population were students. Projected expansion of numbers participating in higher education will further add to these figures.

Employment change

On the economic front, the Bristol economy as a whole has, historically, performed strongly. Total employment in the city-region has expanded at an increasing rate in successive decades since 1971, with the rate of growth in the 1980s and 1990s just ahead of national growth rates (Table 2.6). Employment grew by an estimated 15% in the decade leading to 2001, compared with national growth of 14%. Employment growth has been particularly spectacular in South Gloucestershire: up by 24% in the decade to 1991 and an estimated 42% in the decade to 2001.

Bristol City, at the core of the urban area, lost jobs to some extent in the 1970s – down by around 2.5% (1971-81). This was reversed, however, in the 1980s and 1990s, decades which saw significant employment growth, albeit well short of rates for the area as a whole.

As noted earlier in this chapter, the economic performance of certain urban areas has been particularly affected by their legacy in terms of industrial structure and by their ability to capture new expanding industrial sectors. Cities dominated by older manufacturing industries, such as coal and shipbuilding, were particularly hard hit by the rapid contraction of these sectors from the 1970s onwards. Historically, in the early 1970s, a third of all employment in the Bristol city-region was in manufacturing, marginally higher in fact than the

share of manufacturing nationally (Table 2.7). Construction, distribution and transport together accounted for another third of employment locally, little different from their share of national employment. Public sector services including health and education accounted for nearly a quarter of employment locally, slightly up on the national share, reflecting Bristol's role as subregional and regional centre. Business and financial services, mainly representing private sector employment, accounted for less than 6% of employment locally, compared with nearly 12% nationally. In common with many urban areas, Bristol was potentially very vulnerable to manufacturing decline.

As elsewhere in Britain during the 1970s and 1980s, there were major transformations in the industrial structure of the Bristol city-region. In some respects, including the decline of traditional manufacturing sectors, these mirrored national trends. Manufacturing employment in the Bristol city-region was almost halved over the 20-year period from 1971 to 1991, with major job losses in the city's traditional manufacturing sectors, including tobacco, paper and packaging and aerospace (Table 2.8). While this clearly had major implications for the economy and employment locally, the overall scale of manufacturing decline was no more severe than that for the country as a whole, and less severe than in many other localities over this period.

Business and financial services, on the other hand, grew rapidly in the 1970s and 1980s, expanding their share of employment in the Bristol city-region from just under 6% in 1971 to nearly 16% by 1991. There was strong growth nationally in business and financial services over this period with employment up by nearly 30% in the 1970s and over 40% in the 1980s. This was far outpaced locally with employment in

Table 2.6: Total employment (1981-2001)

	1981	1991	2001	1981-91 (%)	1991-2001 (%)
Bath and NE Somerset	67,900	77,124	81,200	13.6	5.3
Bristol City	211,170	224,258	228,500	6.2	1.9
North Somerset	51,780	61,866	79,250	19.5	28.1
South Gloucestershire	80,260	99,252	141,310	23.7	42.4
Bristol city-region	411,110	462,500	530,260	12.5	14.7
Britain (000s)	435,598	488,460	556,973	12.1	14.0

Note: Includes employees and self-employed.
Source: Joint Strategic Planning and Transportation Unit, Bristol, estimates based on Annual Employment Statistics and Annual Business Inquiry, National Statistics, adjusted for known errors

Table 2.7: Employment by sector, Bristol city-region and UK (1971-91) (%)

| | 1971 % of total | 1981 % of total | 1991 % of total | 1971 % of total | 1981 % of total | 1991 % of total |
	Bristol city-region			UK		
Agriculture, energy, water	3.6	3.6	2.9	6.5	5.5	3.7
Manufacturing	33.2	26.9	18.3	31.3	24.2	17.7
Construction	7.4	6.6	7.4	6.5	6.4	7.3
Distribution, transport etc	26.5	26.6	27.1	25.4	26.9	27.5
Business and miscellaneous services	5.6	8.6	15.8	11.6	14.9	19.8
Public admin, education, health	23.1	26.7	28.5	18.7	22.0	24.1
All industries	100	100	100	100	100	100
All industries (total)	401,100	411,100	462,705	24,482,000	24,488,000	25,960,000

Source: Census of Population, OPCS

Table 2.8: Employment change by sector, Bristol city-region and UK (1971-91) (%)

| | Bristol city-region | UK | Bristol city-region | UK |
	1971-81		1981-91	
Agriculture, energy, water	2.1	−14.7	−9.6	−28.6
Manufacturing	−16.9	−22.4	−23.3	−22.8
Construction	−8.6	−1.5	25.1	19.3
Distribution, transport, etc	2.9	5.7	14.6	8.7
Business and miscellaneous services	56.8	28.9	107.0	40.6
Public admin, education, health	18.8	17.6	19.9	15.9
All industries	2.5	0.0	12.6	6.0

Source: Census of Population, OPCS

the Bristol city-region, up by 57% in the 1970s and doubling in the 1980s.

In addition, there was significant growth locally in public sector services, including health and education, over the same period and some growth in transport and distribution. Local rates of growth in these sectors largely mirrored national rates, however. Thus, they were significant in terms of overall job growth. There was, however, little change in their significance locally compared with the national picture.

It was, above all, the strong performance of the local economy in terms of growth in private sector services that accounted for the competitive strength of the Bristol city-region at the start of the 1990s. In crude terms, around 48,000 manufacturing jobs were lost in the 20 years to 1991, offset numerically at least by a gain of 51,000 jobs in business and financial services. Overall job growth was further boosted by an additional 58,000 jobs in other service activities.

More recently, the 1990s saw these broad trends continue (Table 2.8). By 2001, manufacturing had fallen to just 12.5% of employment in the Bristol city-region and was then significantly below the national figure of just over 14%. There was also significant decline in manufacturing locally in the early 1990s, but some indication of recovery as the economy strengthened in the second half of the decade (statistics relating to manufacturing are somewhat unreliable, however).

Locally, banking, finance and insurance continued to outpace growth nationally. By 2001, the sector accounted for over 22% of all employment in the city-region, compared with less than 20% in the country as a whole (Table 2.9). Significant growth continued in the latter part of the 1990s across a range of other service activities including transport and communications, public administration, health and education, distribution, hotels and restaurants. There was also rapid growth in construction employment from a low base. Rates of growth locally were roughly comparable with national trends. Unexceptional compared to national trends,

Table 2.9: Employment by industrial sector and area (2001) (%)

	Bristol City	South Gloucsestershire	Bristol city-region	Britain
1 Agriculture and fishing	–	0.1	0.1	1.0
2 Energy and water	0.6	1.1	0.7	0.8
3 Manufacturing	11	15.8	12.5	14.2
4 Construction	4.8	6.6	5.2	4.5
5 Distribution, hotels and restaurants	20.6	24.9	23.7	24.3
6 Transport and communications	5.2	9.1	6.2	6.1
7 Banking, finance and insurance, etc	28.3	15.4	21.7	19.6
8 Public admin, education and health	24.6	23.6	25.7	24.3
9 Other services	4.9	3.2	4.3	5.2
Total (000s)	231,817	114,755	488,711	25,456,397

Source: National Statistics (NOMIS), Annual Business Inquiry.
Note: Statistics are based on a sample of establishments and subject to variation between time periods, and should be regarded as approximate. Excludes self-employed. Excludes Agriculture Class 001.

they did nevertheless account for significant growth in employment locally in absolute terms.

Comparing sub-areas, there are significant differences between Bristol City and South Gloucestershire, the latter including the major concentration of employment in the 'north fringe'. In terms of sectoral change, statistics on manufacturing for sub-areas locally are somewhat unreliable and must be treated with caution. Across the full range of service sector activities, however, growth rates in South Gloucestershire were well above average for the area as a whole and well ahead of those for Bristol City. This suggests some closing of the gap on Bristol City in terms of its share of financial services employment and public sector services. There was also particularly rapid growth in South Gloucestershire's distribution, hotels and restaurants and in transport and communications.

South Gloucestershire has an above-average share of manufacturing employment compared with the Bristol city-region as a whole, and Bristol a below-average share (Table 2.8). A major factor here is the concentration of aerospace and high technology manufacturing in the north fringe. It also has above-average employment in distribution and in transport and communications reflecting both a concentration of warehousing and related activities adjacent to the M4/M5 junction and the growth of the regional shopping and leisure complex at Cribbs Causeway.

Bristol City has a significantly above-average share of employment in banking, finance and insurance

reflecting the continuing strength of the core urban area in these activities. Its share of employment in other sectors is average or below average for all other sectors, emphasising the central key importance of financial services to this part of the city-region. It accounts for 28% of all jobs in the core urban area.

Again comparing sub-areas, in overall terms, employment growth in South Gloucestershire continued to outpace that of Bristol City in the most recent period, 1995-2001 (Table 2.10). Employment in South Gloucestershire grew rapidly, by around 23% over this period, compared with 10% in Bristol City. Again, however, the modest but continuing growth of employment in overall terms in Bristol City, at the core of the urban area as a whole, should be noted; it runs counter to any trend towards 'de-urbanisation' of employment.

The relative competitiveness and overall performance of a particular urban area can, to some extent, be understood in terms of those economic activities which are particularly important to it. Importance in terms of absolute numbers employed is one aspect. This, however, in part relates to the scale of the urban area. Much employment and economic activity, particularly in the service sector, simply relates to the size of the local population and to the general scale of economic activity locally, supplying and servicing businesses and households in the area.

The importance of particular activities in employment terms can also be measured relative to the national picture, by measuring which activities

Table 2.10: Employment change by industrial sector and area (1995-2001)

	Bristol city-region		Bristol		South Gloucestershire		Britain
	No	**%**	**No**	**%**	**No**	**%**	**%**
1 Agriculture and fishing	–	–	–	–	–	–	–12.4
2 Energy and water	–	–	–	–	–	–	–9.9
3 Manufacturing	5,392	9.7	4,970	24.2	110	–6.2	–9.8
4 Construction	8,324	48.8	3,066	38.3	2,823	9.7	27.5
5 Distribution, hotels and restaurants	18,573	19.1	4,278	9.8	8,205	35.2	15.3
6 Transport and communications	5,521	22.1	–1,643	–12.0	5,155	60.9	15.9
7 Banking, finance and insurance, etc	11,575	12.3	4,909	8.1	3,139	16.9	23.8
8 Public admin, education and health	15,779	14.4	6,752	13.5	7,592	38.4	12.1
9 Other services	1,622	8.4	142	1.3	1,266	10.5	25.2
Total	62,653	14.7	21844	10.4	28077	23.3	12.0

Notes: Statistics are based on a sample of establishments and subject to variation between time periods, and should be regarded as approximate. Excludes self-employed. Local statistics for Groups 1 and 2 suppressed due to small numbers and likely sampling error.
Source: National Statistics, Annual Employment Survey (AES) Adjusted Series (1995); Annual Business Inquiry (ABI) (2001)

account for a significantly higher share of employment locally than they do nationally. This can be measured by a 'specialisation index': a value of 1.0 for a particular sector indicates that it accounts for a similar share of employment locally as it does nationally; the higher the value above 1.0, the greater the degree of specialisation locally in that sector (Table 2.11).

A further distinction can be made between activities which sell or export their product or service beyond the urban area itself, increasing employment and income locally, and those which provide mainly for local consumption by households, businesses and other organisations[3]. There is no simple indicator of 'export' orientation. Local sectors and individual businesses may also relate to both local, regional and national or international markets to different degrees.

'Export' activities are particularly important to local economic competitiveness. The scale and quality of goods and services provided for local consumption is also important, however. It is not neutral in terms of growth and competitiveness as sometimes suggested. For example, it impacts in terms of productivity, the attraction of investment, education and skills, quality of life and capacity to attract labour.

In terms of overall scale and a significant degree of export orientation, key sectors in the Bristol city-region include financial services, higher education, telecommunications, software and computing, for example. They also include older specialist sectors such as paper and board, and manufacture of food, beverages and tobacco, now much reduced in size. Aerospace, also reduced in size compared to historic levels of employment, remains particularly significant both in terms of absolute employment and relative to the national picture.

Other major sectors showing some degree of concentration reflect the scale of the urban area and to some degree its subregional or regional role (Table 2.12). Health, employing 32,000, is a particularly significant example of this. Retailing, employing 51,000 (and a further 13,000 in wholesale) caters largely for a local market. However, it also has to some extent a sub-regional or regional catchment in some cases.

Much employment overall is in sectors with lower degrees of concentration or which do not stand out as important relative to the national picture, however (Table 2.12). Many major sectors cater largely for the local population including, for example, school-based and further education employing 31,000 people and social work, 18,000. Bars and restaurants (employing 18,000 people) cater largely for a local market together with a wider visitor market.

---

[3] Business surveys and other forms of local intelligence can give an indication of which sectors and businesses relate more to export rather than local markets.

Table 2.11: Employment specialisation by sector, Bristol city-region (2001)

Industry		Employment	Index of specialisation
752	Provision of services etc	14,815	1.59
803	Higher education	12,825	1.44
353	Manufacture of aircraft and spacecraft	10,632	5.31
747	Industrial cleaning	9,661	1.24
660	Insurance and pension funding	9,237	2.23
641	Post and courier activities	7,833	1.4
742	Architectural/engineering activities etc	7,723	1.31
642	Telecommunications	6,392	1.34
672	Activities auxiliary to insurance/pensions	4,620	1.79
222	Printing etc	4,347	1.22
285	Treatment and coating of metals etc	3,880	1.54
746	Investigation and security activities	3,842	1.4
726	Other computer-related activities	3,206	1.45
922	Radio and television activities	2,229	1.49
744	Advertising	2,126	1.22
713	Renting of other machinery and equipment	1,996	1.31
212	Manufacture: articles of paper/paperboard	1,874	1.41
300	Manufacture: office machinery/computers	1,769	2.14
711	Renting of automobiles	1,142	1.92
266	Manufacture of articles of concrete etc	1,126	1.94
921	Motion picture and video activities	1,042	1.38
297	Manufacture of domestic appliances not elsewhere specified	–	1.78

Notes: Shows all sectors at three-digit Standard Industrial Classification (SIC) level with more than 1,000 employees and with a location quotient (LQ) of 1.2 or above. The location quotient (LQ) measures the percentage share of employment in a given sector locally relative to the percentage share nationally (LQ = Local %/National %). An LQ of more than 1.0 for a given sector thus indicates a higher proportion of total employment in that sector locally than nationally.

Source: NOMIS, National Statistics, Annual Business Inquiry (2001)

As elsewhere in the country, a relatively small number of large-scale businesses in the Bristol city-region account for a large proportion of total employment. Less than 1% of establishments locally, only 300 in total, have more than 200 employees. Yet these 300 account for nearly a third of all employment locally (Table 2.13). Just 4% of establishments, 1,600 in all, account for well over half of all employment. Thus, the fortunes and performance of a relatively small proportion of all establishments in the local area determine, to a large extent, the overall competitiveness and performance of the area as a whole. The 30 largest individual employers locally are shown in Table 2.14. As the list shows, many of these are large, relatively stable employers serving the local population – the local authorities and health trusts in particular, together with major retailers. However, the list also includes the large 'export' oriented employers which are crucial to the overall competitive success of the subregional economy – the financial services sector, the Ministry of Defence (MoD), companies such as

Orange, Rolls-Royce and Airbus UK, as well as the city-region's three universities.

As details of the 30 largest employers indicate, a significant proportion of the larger employers, particularly in the public sector, are essentially location-fixed. Employment and investment may vary over time, but usually within relatively narrow bounds, reflecting shifts in emphasis in terms of public expenditure and public policy. Possibly half of the largest 20 employers fall into this category.

Significant change in terms of employment and investment locally is likely, therefore, to be determined by the decisions of a relatively small number of mainly private sector establishments or by their parent companies. Corporate strategy and restructuring will potentially be reflected in investment and expansion, dis-investment and downsizing or possibly relocation.

Bristol's economic strength and its capacity to adapt over time relate to a combination of factors. Current

Table 2.12: Other major employment sectors, Bristol city-region (2001)

Industry		Employment	Index of specialisation
851	Human health activities	31,626	0.95
521	Retail sale in non-specialised stores	27,078	1.14
524	Other: new goods in specialised stores	23,645	1.1
801	Primary education	17,911	1.09
853	Social work activities	17,656	0.95
452	Building of complete constructions etc	14,645	1.14
745	Labour recruitment etc	13,991	1.03
802	Secondary education	13,220	1.13
741	Accounting/book-keeping activities etc	13,046	0.9
751	Administration of the state etc	12,816	0.91
651	Monetary intermediation	9,883	1.07
554	Bars	9,438	0.92
553	Restaurants	9,020	0.89
602	Other land transport	8,516	0.94
748	Miscellaneous business activities not elsewhere specified	6,807	0.94
453	Building installation	6,056	1.17
722	Software consultancy and supply	5,854	1.05
551	Hotels	5,106	0.89
515	Wholesale of non-agricultural products etc	4,233	0.94
513	Wholesale of food, beverages and tobacco	4,211	1.13
930	Other service activities	4,149	0.68
501	Sale of motor vehicles	4,129	0.94
514	Wholesale of household goods	4,025	0.79
522	Retail: food, etc in specialised stores	3,967	0.91
516	Wholesale of machinery, equipment etc	3,910	0.82
926	Sporting activities	3,900	0.8
252	Manufacture of plastic products	3,804	1.09
454	Building completion	3,715	1.14
502	Maintenance and repair of motor vehicles	3,581	1.11
555	Canteens and catering	3,532	0.71
221	Publishing	3,217	1.08
913	Activities: other membership organisations	3,213	1.02
804	Adult and other education	2,918	0.76
158	Manufacture of other food products	2,566	0.71
633	Activities of travel agencies etc not elsewhere specified	2,426	1.01
703	Real estate activities	2,409	0.88
503	Sale of motor vehicle parts/accessories	2,083	1.15

Notes: Shows all sectors at three-digit SIC level with more than 2,000 employees and LQs of less than 1.2. These sectors are thus large in absolute terms but do not account for a particularly large share of employment locally compared with the country as a whole.
Source: NOMIS, National Statistics, Annual Business Inquiry (ABI) (2001)

Table 2.13: Employment by size of establishment, Bristol city-region (2001)

Number of employees	1-10	11-49	50-199	200+	Total
Number of establishments	33,067	5,284	1,297	305	40,212
% of all establishments	82.8	13.2	3.2	0.8	100.0
Employment	95,848	120,136	117,512	155,215	488,711
% of total employment	19.6	24.6	24.0	31.8	100.0

Source: NOMIS, National Statistics, Annual Business Inquiry (ABI) (2001)

Table 2.14: Thirty largest employers in Bristol city-region (2002)

Employer	Location	Employees	Activity
Bristol City Council	Central Bristol	16,500	Local government
South Gloucestershire Council	South Gloucestershire	9,500	Local government
Ministry of Defence	South Gloucestershire and Bath	9,000	Government ministry
North Bristol NHS Trust	South Gloucestershire	8,100	Health trust
Bath & North East Somerset Council	Bath, various	6,500	Local government
North Somerset Council	Weston-super-Mare, various	6,300	Local government
United Bristol Healthcare Trust	Central Bristol	6,000	Health trust
University of Bristol	Bristol	5,000	University
Nat West/Royal Bank of Scotland/Direct Line	Central Bristol, Aztec West	4,700	Banking, insurance
Airbus UK	Filton	4,650	Aerospace – wing technology
Rolls-Royce	Patchway	3,940	Aerospace – military engines
University of the West of England	Frenchay	3,500	University
British Telecom	Central Bristol	3,200	Telecommunications
Consignia	Patchway (HQ), various	3,000	Postal services
Avon & Somerset Police	Portishead (HQ), various	3,000	Police
Orange	South Gloucestershire, Bristol	3,000	Telecommunications – mobile phone network
Bristol & West Building Society	Central Bristol	2,600	Building Society/Bank
AXA Sun Life	Stoke Gifford, Central Bristol	2,500	Insurance
Lloyds TSB	Central Bristol (HQ), various	2,500	Banking services
Somerfield	Whitchurch (HQ), various	2,500	Retail – supermarkets
Asda Stores	Various	2,500	Retail – supermarkets
Tesco	Various	2,500	Retail – supermarkets
Sainsbury	Various	2,500	Retail – supermarkets
Bath Royal United Health Trust	Bath	2,400	Health trust
University of Bath	Bath	2,000	University
Safeway Stores	Various	2,000	Retail – supermarkets
Weston Area Health Trust	Weston-super-Mare	1,850	Health trust
First City Bus/First Badgerline	Various	1,800	Bus services
Clerical Medical	Central Bristol, Clevedon	1,500	Insurance
Royal & Sun Alliance Group	Central Bristol, Clevedon	1,500	Insurance

Note: Figures rounded to the nearest hundred.
Source: Compiled by South Gloucestershire Council (August 2002)

strengths in some sectors reflect location decisions rooted in history – aerospace, printing, packaging and publishing (related historically to the tobacco industry), the BBC and even the University of Bristol would be examples. The American economist Paul Krugman (1994) emphasises the importance of persistent effects of what may be in effect historical accidents, even though a range of different factors then come into play over time[4].

Historically as well, Bristol has attracted significant volumes of inwards investment – financial services from the early 1970s on, Hewlett Packard, Orange and the MoD more recently being key examples. Subsequent expansion of these and many other smaller companies has been a major contributor to economic prosperity locally. The research evidence shows that key influences on the competitive success of Bristol include the importance of a relatively conventional set of location factors contributing to the business environment of the city-region. These have included:

- proximity to London – the recent study of factors contributing to the long-term growth of urban areas identified the clear importance of proximity

---

[4] Krugman terms these persistent effects 'path dependency' or 'qwerty economics', by analogy with the historic layout of the typewriter keyboard which persists to this day.

to London as a significant factor explaining growth (Begg et al, 2002);

- more generally, good motorway and rail links including access to London, the rest of the South East and Heathrow – facilitating both the movement of goods and contact and networking with collaborators and customers within and outside companies, both domestic and international;
- the attractiveness of the city and surrounding area particularly for more senior professional, technical and managerial staff, facilitating initial relocation of key staff and subsequent recruitment and retention;
- the scale and quality of the labour supply including both the local catchment and the capacity to recruit from along the M4 corridor and nationally;
- the availability and cost of premises (relative to London and the South East), particularly in the 1970s relocation boom (coupled with the operation of the Office Development Permit system);
- the availability of major sites for relocation within the city-region, both centrally and particularly on the north fringe adjacent to the M4/M5 interchange.

Unemployment

Again reflecting the economic buoyancy and competitive success of the Bristol city-region, unemployment is significantly below the national rate and has been so throughout the 1990s. At 1.9% by March 2002 (claimant count), it has come down to levels which are sometimes talked of as representing 'full employment'[5]. Alternative measures of unemployment would put the absolute level higher, but in a relatively tight labour market 'hidden' unemployment tends to be lower.

---

[5] Claimant count unemployment figures are presented in order to allow comparison between sub-areas within the city-region. International Labour Organisation (ILO) unemployment is a preferable measure, but sample size for the Labour Force Survey on which it is based does not allow dis-aggregation below the equivalent of county level. At local authority level, rates are only available based on resident working-age population rather than the preferable workplace-based measure. However, this does allow for comparison between local authorities on a uniform basis.

Figure 2.2: Unemployment: Britain, Bristol and South Gloucestershire (1996-2003) (%)

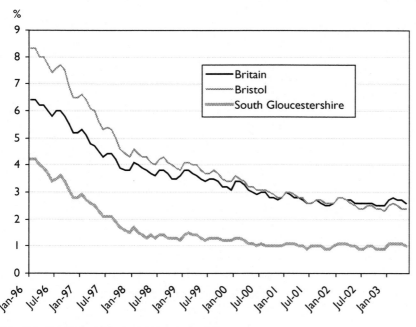

Notes: Rate based on resident working age population.
Source: National Statistics, NOMIS, monthly claimant count

Table 2.15: Unemployment (3 May 2003)

	Total unemployed	Unemployment rate (%)
Bath and NE Somerset	1,266	1.2
Bristol City	5,971	2.4
North Somerset	1,336	1.2
South Gloucestershire	1,572	1.0
Britain	923,954	2.6

Notes: Rate based on resident working-age population.
Source: National Statistics, NOMIS, monthly claimant count

There are significant contrasts between sub-areas (Table 2.15), however, with the unemployment rate in Bristol City at 2.4%, significantly above that for the Bristol city-region as a whole, and that for the other three unitary authorities significantly below the Bristol city-region rate. At May 2003, unemployment in South Gloucestershire at 1.0% was virtually half that for Bristol City.

Comparing local and national rates, unemployment in Bristol City was marginally higher than the national rate in the mid-1990s (Figure 2.2). It then dropped below the national rate in late 1996 and has remained lower since then. Unemployment in South Gloucestershire has been consistently significantly below national rates over the same period. More recently, the difference narrowed slightly, reflecting the fact that the rate in South Gloucestershire was approaching an irreducible residual level.

Despite its overall success in economic terms, reflected in relatively low rates of unemployment, the city-region as a whole has marked spatial concentrations of unemployment, poverty and deprivation even by national standards. This is explored in detail in Chapter 6.

Benchmarking Bristol

Bristol's overall performance can be usefully set in context by benchmarking it against that of other cities both nationally and on a Europe-wide basis. A study of longer-term change in employment over the period 1959-97 found that Bristol city-region grew by 41%, well ahead of employment growth nationally, at 14%.(Britain) and 12% for 'free-standing' cities (Begg et al, 2002). It was ranked 28th out of 78 urban areas nationally (excluding official new and expanded towns). Most of the faster growers were smaller towns and cities in the south of

the country. They also included larger urban areas, with North Hampshire (the Basingstoke/ Farnborough area) and Cambridge in first and second places overall. Of the larger urban areas, Southampton (17th) and Portsmouth (27th) were also ahead of Bristol. Interestingly in a regional context, Exeter grew by nearly 89% over this same period, placing it eighth fastest nationally, and Torbay/Paignton by 51%. Bournemouth/Poole (45%) was also just ahead of Bristol, as was Swindon which virtually doubled in size in employment terms over this same period, but, benefited in the early years in part from official 'expanded town' status.

Finally, a recent study of trends in output, measured as annual rate of growth in GDP per capita, put Bristol 26th out of 121 large city-regions across the 12 members states of the EU. It was not quite in the same league growth-wise as the top performers among major European cities such as Dublin (3rd), Frankfurt (4th), Rome (6th), Munich (7th) or Madrid (9th), or smaller places such as Porto (1st) or Padua (2nd). It was, however, the best-performing UK city after Edinburgh (5th) and in the top quarter of all European city-regions (Cheshire and Magrini, 2002)[6].

Future prospects

Government projections see continuing growth in the Bristol city-region in terms of population and household numbers, significantly ahead of national levels (but slightly less than for the South West as a whole).

Population across the city-region is expected to grow by 81,000 (that is, 8%) over the period 2001-21, compared with only 5% nationally, and only slightly less than compared with the 1990s (Table 2.16). Household growth is forecast at 71,000 (or 16%), a double increase in population numbers and again only slightly down on the 1990s. This clearly represents continuing major expansion in the total

---

[6] Figures are for OECD-defined Functional Urban Regions, for the period 1978/80-1992/94, annual growth rate in GDP per capita. Figures for 1985/87-1995/97 put Bristol even higher at 15th. However, due to the manner in which they are compiled, they are considered less reliable.

Table 2.16: Projections of population and households: Bristol city-region, the South West and England (2001-21)

	Bristol city-region		South West (%)	England (%)
	Number	%		
Household change 2001-21	71,000	16.3	18.9	14
Population change 2001-21	80,900	8.0	9.5	5.2

Source: ONS 1996-based population projections; DTLR-based household projections

number of households that will continue to generate significant pressures in the housing market.

Mindful of this, the government recently rejected the level of new house building proposed by the four local authorities for the period 1996-2011 as part of the Structure Plan process, insisting it was too low to meet demand. The original draft Structure Plan made provision for 43,000 new dwellings. The government eventually accepted a revised figure of 50,200 – a compromise on the figure of 54,300 proposed by the panel at the Plan's Examination in Public in March 1999. Nevertheless, this implies construction of over 16,000 new houses in South Gloucestershire by 2011, just under 15,000 in North Somerset and a further 13,000 in Bristol.

Economic forecasts also suggest continuing growth in employment and output. Overall levels of growth will clearly be driven to a large extent by the strength of the national and international economy. Recent forecasts, nevertheless, see growth in the city-region as a whole significantly up on national growth rates. Output is expected to increase by around 2.5-3.0% per annum (Cambridge Econometrics, 2002). Estimates of employment growth, harder to predict at this sort of scale, vary from 0.5% per annum up to 1.4%[7]. This compares with an achieved rate of 1.2% per annum in the 1980s and 1.7% per annum in the 1990s. The upper estimate for employment growth is not inconceivable, therefore, but earlier growth rates of this magnitude reflected in particular the spectacular growth of north-fringe employment, which is unlikely to be replicated in the current decade or so.

Current forecasts, however, put the city-region as a whole as the 10th fastest growing county (or former county) in terms of output over the period 2000-15. This is bettered only by Berkshire (1st place), Hertfordshire, Buckinghamshire, Oxford and Surrey (all in the South East region); the neighbouring counties of Cambridge and Suffolk in East Anglia; and Wiltshire and Shropshire (Cambridge Econometrics, 2002). The same forecast puts the city-region 12th fastest in terms of employment growth over the same period. Bristol, therefore, is well up there with the acknowledged booming economies of southern England.

---

[7] Cambridge Econometrics (2002) predicted 0.5% per annum in the period 2000-15. A forecast by Warwick University, produced for this study, predicted average growth of 1.4% per annum in the period 2000-10.

3

Reshaping the city

Christine Lambert and Ian Smith

There have been significant changes in the spatial logic of the British economy in the last 30 years at a number of different levels. More recently, at the regional level, the long-standing north/south divergence in growth rates has been reinforced, if anything. This reflects the manufacturing-to-services shift in the economy, the key role of London and the South East region in the 'new knowledge economy' (financial and business services, research and development, and technologically advanced manufacturing), and the environmental attractions of the south to a more mobile and affluent population. Coupled with this, there are strong processes of decentralisation of employment, away from the largest cities and towards suburban and fringe areas and smaller towns (Breheny, 1999; Turok and Edge, 1999; Begg et al, 2001), and this process is especially marked in the London city-region. Despite global pre-eminence, London lost employment in the 1990s. However, the buoyancy of the London economy can be seen, nevertheless, in the spread of metropolitan influence and high employment growth rates in accessible small- and medium-sized towns in the Greater South East, with particular pressures in growth corridors on the national motorway network extending out of London.

Changing urban form in the UK

In addition to these regional and urban differences in economic performance and growth rates, there has been substantial debate about the restructuring of urban form in the context of the post-industrial, post-Fordist economy. Much of the literature on this is North American in origin, and therefore reflects the particular cultural and policy/legal context of the

US, but it nevertheless makes claims to be representing a new and universal urbanisation process (Soja, 2000). In a European context Hall (1995, 1997) and Kloosterman and Musterd (2001) have drawn attention to the complex patterns of decentralisation around global cities such as London, and the inadequacy of the standard monocentric model in describing the contemporary city. The general gist of the argument about the restructuring of contemporary urban form is that the traditional monocentric city has been replaced by a more fragmented and polycentric city-region, extending over a much wider area. The decentralisation of population over a long period, seemingly expressive of strong anti-urban residential preferences, together with growing levels of car ownership and greater mobility, accounts for the extended commuting area around major centres of employment. In addition, a variety of employment uses have dispersed to locations away from the traditional CBD, creating a mosaic of specialised sub-centres networked over a wider city-region and beyond. This, in turn, is related to the fact that, in a post-industrial economy, businesses engaged in processing knowledge and information face a rather different set of options and constraints with respect to their location than do goods-handling activities.

It is suggested that decentralising moves of employment are driven by a variety of factors that encompass property-related reasons, transport and accessibility and the environmental or social characteristics of places. The shift to more space-extensive modes of production and technologies and an easier development process on greenfield land have increased the attraction of locations beyond the urban boundary for a wide variety of activities, including manufacturing, distribution, some office-based functions and space-extensive public services, such as hospitals. A high dependence on road-based movement of goods and for business travel increases the attraction of locations with good motorway access for both distribution and office-based activities. Advances in communications technology have also allowed office-based and information processing functions, and increasingly telemediated consumer services, to take advantage of cheaper locations and lower labour costs away from the urban core. Research and development, high-technology production and higher-order functions may be drawn to high amenity attractive environments, with the attractions of ex-urban locations reinforced by the residential preferences of skilled professional and technical workers (Gillespie, 1999). However, despite the broader evidence of strong decentralising trends, key aspects of employment – notably in financial, business and professional services – remain concentrated in the centres of the largest cities. For these sectors, the attractions of city centres include the social milieu of the city centre and the linkages that large cities offer to other industries and sources of expertise. High-value producer services also have the ability to dominate competition for land and property at the centres of large cities in order to gain access to these advantages of agglomeration. City centres, however, may no longer be the sole – nor even the most important – cluster of economic activity in a city-region; rather, they are part of a wider spatial division of labour, with significant clusters developing elsewhere, notably adjacent to the motorway network (Kloosterman and Musterd, 2001).

The impact of these trends on changing urban form is also mediated by land-use planning policies, which regulate the process of urbanisation in important ways. A commitment to urban containment is a long-standing feature of planning policy in the UK (Hall et al, 1973), operated through formal constraints such as green-belt policy and more general controls on development in the open countryside outside of established settlements. In the 1980s there were attempts to dilute the regulatory role of planning, and the culture and practices of planning shifted to put more emphasis on facilitating a market-driven development process. Specific reforms included Urban Development Corporations in some areas, and a general weakening of planning controls over different 'classes' of development, effectively reducing the scope to control the type (production versus office-based) of employment development. This pro-market policy agenda was mainly pursued, however, through the planning appeals system and via central government intervention in relation to development targets set in structure plans.

However, the era of deregulation in planning terms proved to be fairly short-lived. By the beginning of the 1990s, the benefits of planning in terms of certainty and environmental protection were again recognised, reinforced by the growing political significance of the environmental agenda at national and international level (Allmendinger and Thomas, 1998). The long-standing policy commitment to urban containment has, if anything, been reinforced more recently in the context of a broader commitment to more sustainable development. National planning guidance is promoting more compact forms of urban development, which generate fewer and shorter journeys (DETR, 1994). Most of the policy debate focuses on housing, however, with specific targets for new housing development on brownfield land within urban areas, and higher housing densities (DETR, 2000b). Nevertheless, in practice, the planning system has accommodated a decentralised pattern of growth, either through extensions to existing urban areas or through more dispersed development in rural areas (Bibby and Shepherd, 2001). In the past, planning itself positively facilitated a process of so-called 'concentrated decentralisation', through the new and expanded towns programme, for example. More recently, a market-driven development process has dominated, and urban dispersal has taken more varied and generalised forms.

One impact of changes in the spatial organisation of city-regions is in terms of transport and movement, a key element in policy debates concerning land-use planning and sustainable development. This refers not just to more extended commuting hinterlands, as a consequence of population decentralisation, but also to more complex patterns of movement, including reverse commuting and suburb-to-suburb commuting, as a consequence of employment dispersal. It is also suggested that changes in household career structures, with more dual-career households, is leading to longer-distance commuting as a substitute for migration among this group (Green et al, 1999). The important point about this is that it undermines the idea of self-containment in housing and labour market terms at the level of the individual settlement, an idea that is increasingly promoted in planning debates. Breheny (1999, p 212), for example, characterises the current promotion of self-containment at the settlement level as a "forlorn hope".

The empirical outcomes of economic restructuring in terms of the reorganisation of the space of the city-region, and the specificities of urban form and the character and design of the built environment, are likely to vary between different cities. This will reflect the particular combination of local economic and demographic trends, investment in infrastructure and property development and local planning policies and regimes, as well as the inherited urban structure. However, the literature suggests that it is possible to generalise to some degree about the key features of changing urban form.

It might be anticipated that the strong decentralisation trends, especially in office-based employment and retailing, would undermine city centre areas. While the fortunes of different city centres might vary, the general indications are that the biggest city centres are undergoing a process of rediscovery (Robson et al, 2000b). As discussed earlier, they remain the favoured location for financial, business and professional services, and have an increasingly important role in cultural and leisure services and tourism. In some cities, these new roles are manifested in new flagship developments, including new commercial centres, convention centres, museums and sports stadiums. Such developments have become important symbols of regeneration in many declining industrial cities, often supported by public subsidies or other quasi-public funding sources, such as lottery funding. City centres are also becoming more fashionable as residential environments, with significant new housing development on redeveloped sites or in converted buildings taking place in a number of cities (Robson et al, 2000b). This latter trend is given added impetus by changes in planning and urban policy, placing much stronger emphasis on the use of brownfield land for new housing (Urban Task Force, 1999; DETR, 2000b).

The other key trend, which is currently attracting much controversy as well as political and professional attention, is a more direct effect of decentralising population and employment. This is creeping urbanisation of the accessible countryside around towns and cities. Its effects are most apparent in the south of the country, although are not confined to there. It affects small- and medium-sized towns as well as villages, with planning policies generally restricting much new development in open countryside. Analysis of land-use change statistics indicates that the extent of new urban development is highest in counties in the Greater South East, in formerly mainly rural areas (Bibby and Shepherd, 1995, 2001; Bramley, 1999). There is strong pressure for new housing in much of the south, and most of the policy attention has focused on the impacts of this and the ways in which the pattern of new housing development can be changed. Employment and transport-related uses (essentially roads and car parks) are of almost equal significance, however, in terms of new urban development in these 'high growth' counties, although these tend to attract less attention (Bramley, 1999). This is a long-standing feature of urban change in the UK, and its environmental and social impacts have been examined at length.

A specific aspect of decentralisation that even casual observers of the landscapes around cities will recognise is the development in the last decade or so of out-of town business parks and office complexes, retail outlets and shopping centres, leisure centres and substantial new housing developments. Of course, the expansion of cities through new suburban development has been happening throughout the last century; however, residential uses have more recently been joined by a variety of employment and other uses. Such new zones of growth have a strong association with major road links and motorway interchanges, and were a particular feature of new urban development in the 1980s and early 1990s. They represent a qualitatively new kind of built environment, partly reflecting the different space needs of business and industry noted above. They also depend, as Byrne (2001, p 162) notes, for their creation on the majority of households owning at least one car. Examples can be found along the motorway axes from London in the most economically dynamic regions. However, similar 'edge-of-city' type developments have also been identified in other regions, including the North East (Byrne, 2001), the West Midlands (Lowe, 2000) and central Scotland (Bramley, 1999). While parallels can be drawn with the US concept of 'edge cities' (Garreau, 1991), British examples are typically more much modest in scale. They may also be more a manifestation of general decentralisation and spreading urban influence in the British context, rather than regarded as independent alternatives to the city, as the US literature suggests (Hartshorne and Muller, 1989; Garreau, 1991). For these reasons, the term 'post-suburban' development may be a more appropriate description of these new urban spaces (Hall, 1998).

It is perhaps worth outlining some general features of these new, edge-of-city urban spaces, since the character of the built environment in such locations differs significantly from traditional notions of what a city looks like. The most obvious feature is that development densities tend to be low overall, and edge-of-city development is typically quite dispersed. Much of the land is dedicated to roads and car-parking, and these are the visual features that dominate. Space for pedestrian movement is absent or inadequate, with the engineered road, rather than the street, as the main form of circulation. Edge-of-city development may comprise a mixture of different uses – employment, shopping and leisure as well as new housing – but the pattern of development is often highly segregated, with particular sites dedicated to a single use, separated by relatively large areas of under-utilised land. The configuration of development can frequently involve long, circuitous journeys, which further deters walking as a means of getting around. Individual sites can be well planned and landscaped, and there may be examples of 'spectacular' architecture. Yet the overall impression is of fragmented and rather chaotic development. Edge cities are typically not well served by public transport and are inherently quite difficult to serve, given low densities and dispersed development patterns.

From the point of view of a planning system that is now dedicated to promoting more compact cities, with the aim of reducing car use and minimising the loss of land to development, 'edge-city' type development is clearly very problematic. However, in economic terms, such areas may be highly successful and dynamic.

Changing urban form in the Bristol city-region

As discussed in Chapter 2, in a national context Bristol is a relatively successful and growing city-region. The local economy, however, has undergone substantial restructuring since the 1970s, and this process has been accompanied by significant change in the spatial structure of employment in the city-region. During the 1970s and 1980s, the employment base of the city centre was boosted by the relocation of financial companies to Bristol from London and the South East, facilitated by a high level of new office construction in the city centre. On the other hand, much of the job loss associated with manufacturing and port decline affected industries located in the inner city and in the southern suburbs. Defence-related employment in the aerospace sector, located to the north of the city, fell somewhat during this earlier period, but at nothing like the dramatic rate of decline affecting traditionally dominant sectors, such as tobacco and paper and printing. A growth of employment in computing and research and development activities in the 1980s also boosted employment growth north of the city.

Although this uneven pattern of employment change has been modified more recently, the broad pattern remains the same. Employment in the urban core has grown slowly through the 1990s, with financial and business services continuing to dominate. This is accompanied by a broad pattern of dispersed employment growth in the districts surrounding the city, overlaid by the emergence of a significant new employment centre in the extension to the built-up area reaching into the district of South Gloucestershire, an area known locally as the 'north fringe'. By 1998, there were around 46,000 jobs located in the north fringe, representing an increase of 70% over a 15-year period. To put this figure in context, Bristol city centre has 67,000 employees. The sectors experiencing high levels of growth in the north fringe in the 1990s included retail, financial services, transport and distribution, telecommunications, research and development and higher education. This job growth was associated with a mixture of inward investment from outside the city-region, some decentralisation of businesses within the city and in-situ growth of a number of activities.

The emergence of the north fringe as a significant new employment centre in the city-region originates in strategic policy decisions made in the latter half of the 1970s. Plans prepared by the former Avon County Council recognised the need for additional land release for employment in order to compensate for the decline of manufacturing employment, and also for significant amounts of housing land in the light of demographic forecasts. The potential of the north fringe reflected its good communications at the western end of the developing M4 corridor, its location adjacent to an important junction on the national motorway network and in close proximity to a high-speed rail link to London, and the substantial amount of undeveloped land. Therefore, the area was seen as a logical expansion area for Bristol in employment and residential development terms. Plans were subsequently confirmed for the release of substantial amounts of employment land and for the designation of 1,000 acres as the location of a major new settlement-scale housing development accommodating 8,500 homes.

Development in the north fringe has been rapid, especially during the late 1980s and through the 1990s. As a consequence, the district of South Gloucestershire has been one of the fastest growing areas in the country. Population grew by 10% in each of the decades 1981-91 and 1991-2001; total employment grew by almost 25% in the 1980s, and by almost 45% in the 1990s. Around 23,000 new homes have been built in the period since 1985, 380,000 square metres of office space has been constructed in the north fringe alone, together with 1.3 million square feet of retail space.

The development in the north fringe includes a university campus, a regional shopping centre, a large government office complex, various business parks and substantial housing developments. Major employers include Hewlett Packard Computing, Orange Telecommunications, plus a variety of smaller companies involved in telecommunications and computing, and representing a wave of inward investment by high-technology firms into the area and some spin-off activity. The Ministry of Defence (MoD) Procurement Division, which consolidated operations formerly scattered across the country, occupies a complex, allegedly the single largest purpose-built office development in Europe, employing 6,000 people. The AXA Sun Life insurance company has relocated its headquarters and 2,500 jobs from the centre of Bristol. UWE, located in the area since the 1960s, has undergone significant expansion, and by the end of the 1990s had more than 20,000 students and employed over 2,000 staff. The Mall regional shopping centre opened in the mid-1990s, and provides over 700,000 square feet of retail space and employs 3,700 people. The Bradley Stoke housing estate, nearing completion at the end of the 1990s, provides 8,500 new homes, housing couples and young families more than any other group.

From an economic point of view, development in this area has done much to strengthen the local economy. The availability of strategic sites of national and international significance has attracted a number of companies operating in world markets, as well as accommodating major domestic inward investment such as that represented by the MoD complex and regional shopping centre. Development in the area has been significant in underpinning the restructuring of the local economy away from declining manufacturing sectors and towards growing service sectors. Yet there have been a number of down sides to this explosion of new urban development. Much of the new development takes the form of low-density, dispersed campus-style business parks and office developments. In physical terms, the north fringe closely resembles the generalised character of 'edge cities' described in the previous section. These physical characteristics, combined with the absence of any concerted effort to plan for and invest in public transport in parallel with the developments taking place, means that most journeys into and around the area are by car. Consequently, it suffers from high levels of traffic growth and growing problems of congestion on the road network.

In contrast to this explosive growth of business-related and housing development at the periphery of the city, the city centre appeared in the early part of the 1990s to be losing out. In the period following the late 1980s property boom, there was very little new commercial or retail investment in the city centre (see Figure 3.1). Moreover, the city centre experienced problems of low demand for office space, high levels of vacancy and falling rents. By the middle of the 1990s, fears were expressed by the City Council that developments in north Bristol were

Figure 3.1: Office completions, Bristol City and Bristol 'out-of-town' (1977-98) (1,000m²)

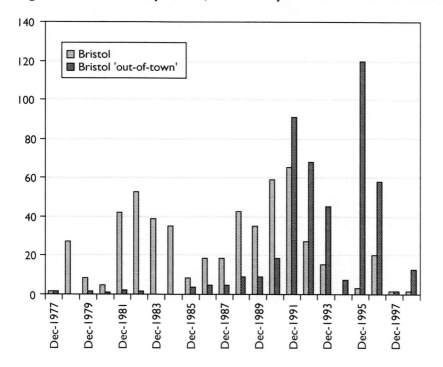

Source: Joint Strategic Planning and Transportation Unit, Bristol

beginning to undermine the social and economic hegemony of the city centre. The grounds for these fears were:

- the relocation of a major financial services employer to a greenfield site on the north fringe;
- the threat that a second major employer, the Bristol and West Building Society, would follow;
- and this, in addition to the approval of The Mall regional shopping centre, and the consequent withdrawal of a major department store from the city's retail core.

However, by the end of the 1990s the property market in the city recovered and a number of significant new development schemes were underway. Bristol Harbourside, being developed for leisure, commercial and residential development, has been underpinned by a successful Millennium lottery bid. Temple Quay, a major new office complex promoted by English Partnerships and the South West Regional Development Agency has been developed adjacent to the city's main railway station, a previously marginal area. Significantly, the Bristol and West Building Society opted to remain in the city centre,

developing a new building at Temple Quay. A significant wave of new city-centre residential development has taken place, through a mixture of redevelopment of vacant sites and conversion of redundant office buildings. Much of this is highly prestigious and expensive housing in waterfront locations, targeted at the affluent consumer, but also important is investment in new student accommodation in the city centre. There has been a substantial development of new leisure uses and hotels, again involving the conversion of obsolete commercial buildings. Plans have also been announced for a major extension of the city-centre retail area.

In spite of the fears that edge-of-city growth would lead to a 'hollowing out' of the city centre, the evidence suggests that latterly the city centre has experienced something of a revival. In employment terms, growth in the urban core is modest compared with peripheral districts in the city-region, but Bristol remains unusual in a national context as a large city that has sustained its employment base (Begg et al, 2001). In population terms, the city has shifted from population decline over a number of decades to modest growth in the 1990s. Population in and around the city centre, however, has grown strongly in the 1990s, with growth rates of 3% per annum, outstripping those in the city as a whole and in the surrounding suburban districts and satellite towns. There are indications, however, of some reorientation of the role of the city centre with a stronger emphasis on residential and consumption uses, replacing to some extent the traditional employment role of the city centre. There are also indications of a move up-market in housing terms, with potential gentrification effects rippling out into neighbouring inner areas.

Explaining the changing shape of the city-region

First, what are the factors that account for the explosive growth that has taken place in the Bristol north fringe? It has already been indicated that the area was designated for major growth because of the potential offered by its location and accessibility. Policy at central and local government level, therefore, played an important role. As far as central government is concerned, investment in transport infrastructure in the 1970s worked in north Bristol's favour by increasing the accessibility of the area, linking the area both to the national motorway network, and to London and the South East via the M4 and railway. This investment, by significantly improving the accessibility of the area to London, Heathrow airport and the rest of the South East, also increased its attraction for businesses looking for locations in the south east, but constrained by a wider context of planning restraint in counties to the west of London. Local policy also facilitated growth and development with the identification of north Bristol as a strategic growth node and subsequent land release. Beyond this, however, local planning policy exercised little control over an essentially market-led development process. During the 1980s and early 1990s, a period of high growth, the area north of Bristol was under the control of a local authority widely perceived to be pro-development, and this local policy stance was also in tune with the deregulation agenda of the Conservative government at national level. A senior planning officer described the area in the mid-1980s as:

... under siege from development pressure ... and this was the era of de-regulation in planning encouraged by central government. Circulars and PPGs were against intervention in development and design control was dismissed as subjective. In transport terms everything we know now was not on the agenda. Developments were usually tested in traffic terms to work out the implications for the road system, but no one talked about restraining car use or cycling. The buses were de-regulated and the assumption was that demand would create supply. Low density, car dependant development was what the market delivered at the time.

The scale of new development in the north fringe is also partly a reflection of inter-jurisdictional conflict and competition between the core city and the periphery. Although physically contiguous with the built-up area of Bristol City, the north fringe has always been administered by a separate authority. During the 1980s, the planning policy stances of Bristol City Council and the neighbouring North Avon district diverged considerably. Bristol at that time was typically seen as suspicious of the private sector and resistant to commercial development (Punter, 1990), while the neighbouring North Avon local authority emphasised a pro-growth, pro-development stance. This difference was widely understood in the property sector locally and influenced the investment strategies of the development industry. There is also evidence that the political leadership of North Avon were engaged in a project to capture development as a way of sustaining the local economy and the employment base. In part, this reflected anxiety locally about the vulnerability of defence industries, the traditional underpinning of the local economy. Competition with the city centre was most obviously expressed, however, in relation to the support locally for the regional shopping centre, against the opposition of the city and county authorities.

However, the wider context of growth in the city-region, combined with changes in the structure of the local economy and the changing land and property and accessibility requirements of business and industry, are important factors in explaining why north Bristol experienced such massive growth. In a survey of the largest employers located in the area (Boddy et al, 1999), the following qualities were identified as influencing their decision to locate in the north fringe[8]. First, the new business parks developed in north Bristol have offered a range of types and sizes of property, opportunities for different rental, leasehold or freehold arrangements, together with the sort of image that many businesses want to project to customers, parent companies and current or potential employees. Second, good motorway access and rail links to London and Heathrow airport are important for employees travelling out and for customers and business partners from elsewhere, particularly those in technologically advanced sectors where product development relies on collaborative working with customers and business partners, within the country or overseas. It is also important in terms of potential labour force catchment, maximising the capacity to draw on the wider M4 corridor labour market, typically described as extending to 45–60 minutes journey time. A number of businesses noted the build-up of IT personnel and, increasingly, specialist telecommunications staff in the M4 corridor. This forms an extended market for recruitment of staff with the possibility of commuting or relocation. Generally speaking then, locations in north Bristol offered a particular package of attributes – sites and premises offering flexibility, image and environment, and access and parking. Many of these businesses also claimed that locations in the central part of the city did not represent a viable alternative.

The same set of factors can also be interpreted as creating the conditions for investment to be diverted away from the city centre in the first half of the 1990s. While direct relocation of businesses from centre to edge has not taken place on a massive scale (the local authorities estimate that around 6,000 jobs in the north fringe represent such a movement), it is likely that some displacement of investment did occur. Expansionary pressures arising in the city centre may have effectively been diverted to out-of-town locations, notably in retailing. Some inward investing companies, faced with a choice of the two locations, are likely to have been influenced by the

relatively unconstrained supply of land and new commercial property in the north fringe. The relative evaluation of the two locations was also influenced by perceptions of the relative accessibility of the city centre as against the north fringe. A long history of under-investment in public transport infrastructure in the city, and growing levels of car-based commuting, have been reflected in increasing business concern about problems of congestion in the city centre. Concerns over transport and accessibility in the city centre remain, although these are now joined by the emerging problems of traffic congestion also in the north fringe.

The processes of decentralisation, however, have led to some devaluation of central area land and buildings, allowing formerly less profitable activities, such as housing, to move into central locations. Coupled with demographic and household changes leading to growth of small households, a buoyant housing market, stronger policy emphasis on urban housing development and shifting consumer preferences, this has facilitated a significant expansion of new housing supply in the city centre. This process has also been underpinned by specific local policy initiatives to promote housing investment in the city centre and a relaxation of planning control over the conversion of employment to other uses. A by-product is that surplus commercial space has been removed from the market, improving the viability of new commercial investment in the city centre. It should also be emphasised, however, that the key new commercial developments in the city centre at Bristol Harbourside and Temple Quay are a product of public–private partnership, and significant subsidy.

The reshaping of the city-region, however, has been associated with growing spatial inequalities, with a marked distinction between a relatively prosperous northern area and areas in the south of the city, suffering manufacturing job loss and economic decline. In spite of the overall context of economic growth and general buoyancy in the city-region, a number of neighbourhoods in the southern suburbs have high and persistent unemployment (see Chapter 6). This is accompanied by a wider problem of sub-regional economic imbalance, with strong population growth in the south of the sub-region outstripping job growth and leading to increasing levels of longer-distance commuting across the sub-region from south to north.

---

[8] The telephone survey was of private sector employers in the Bristol city-region, 300 businesses and in-depth face-to-face interviews with 22 companies (mainly in financial and business services, or information and communications technology). The survey included firms located in the city centre and on the city's northern fringe.

Current issues: managing growth in the city-region

In the latter half of the 1990s there was a change in local government arrangements, as well as in local politics and in local planning policy in the Bristol city-region. This has led to a lively debate over sustainable levels of growth in the city-region and a shift of policy with respect to the fast-expanding Bristol north fringe. Following local government reorganisation in the area in 1996, the strategic level county authority was abolished and replaced by four new unitary authorities. Bristol City itself remains under-bounded, excluding a large portion of the built-up area, including the north fringe growth area. This was in spite of a campaign by business interests and the city council itself, which argued for an enlarged city territory as a more appropriate basis for economic development and strategic land-use and transport planning. Political control in South Gloucestershire, to the north of Bristol, shifted from the Conservatives to the Liberal Democrats. This political group had campaigned specifically to resist further growth in the area, on the grounds that unacceptable environmental impacts had followed, particularly in transport terms, and that physical and community infrastructure had failed to keep up with the level of population and employment growth witnessed.

A new strategic plan for the city-region, prepared jointly by the four unitary authorities, sought to change the distribution of employment growth in the sub-region. In relation to the north fringe, the new strategy states:

> The expansion of employment in the north fringe needs to be restricted and managed: to assist prospects for a more balanced pattern of employment across the plan area; to assist economic regeneration in Bristol; and to help improve transport conditions and the environment of the area.... No further planning permissions therefore should be granted for business park development beyond existing permissions. (JSPTU, 1998, p 80)

The new strategy aims to steer growth to areas south of the sub-region, and to areas better served by public transport than is north Bristol. As well as responding to the local concerns with economic imbalance and

urban regeneration, it is also in line with changing planning policy at central government level, which was placing stronger emphasis on forms of new urban development that contribute to reducing travel by car (DETR, 1994).

The aspirations of the authorities to redirect economic development, however, may be difficult to achieve in practice, implying a significant change in the logic of location for many of the new businesses in the north fringe. Some of the specific attributes that north Bristol offers – a high level of accessibility to London and the South East, together with the labour market assets of the M4 corridor – are difficult to replicate elsewhere. Added to this, the desire of employers and retailers to cater for car-borne employees and customers, the positive 'image' of the out-of-town business park, and the flexibility that new buildings on greenfield sites offer, suggests that in-town locations would not be attractive to some companies. There are tensions also between the city-region objective of reducing employment growth in the north fringe and regional planning and economic development objectives to sustain growth in the Bristol–Swindon corridor as the basis of the economic competitiveness of the wider region (RPG10, 3 February, 2001). The northern part of the South West region is expected to remain the main focus for growth in the South West, and Bristol in particular is seen as having key advantages of status and location in terms of future economic potential. Finally, there are substantial, and yet to be developed, employment land allocations to the north of the city-region, a legacy of the policy stance of the past. These will continue to facilitate employment growth in the area for some time. Despite general anti-growth sentiments described later in this chapter, the local authorities have been unwilling to withdraw the commitment to development of these strategic employment sites. This reinforces that there are significant time lags between changes in planning policy and changes in the pattern and form of development.

In parallel with this debate about the extent to which planning can and should attempt to divert market driven processes in pursuit of more balanced economic development, there is a wider debate about sustainable levels of growth in the sub-region. The controversy here has focused on demographic and household projections in particular, and the housing development implications of these in the city-region. Driven by a mixture of indigenous growth and migration into the area, a consequence of good economic performance, current projections suggest that the number of households will increase by around 70,000 over a 20-year period to 2021. In housing development terms this implies a continuation of past, relatively high, rates of development into the future. Bristol, unlike some of the major English industrial cities, lacks a significant legacy of vacant and derelict land as a consequence of de-industrialisation. As a result the accommodation of growth implies a greater reliance on new urban expansion. However, there are strong anti-growth sentiments in the suburban districts around the city, motivated by political and popular concerns over threats to local environmental quality and the already over-stretched infrastructure of the city-region. The inadequacies of infrastructure in the burgeoning edge of city developments in the city-region, particularly the road network and public transport provision, underlies much of the resistance to growth locally, fuelling the perception that further growth is inevitably negative in its consequences.

Resistance to housing development in particular, combined with a more positive accommodation of economic development, could lead to growing labour scarcity as a result of inadequate provision of housing relative to job growth (see Bramley and Lambert, 2002). Alternatively, adjustment implies increased levels of longer-distance commuting, contributing to higher traffic growth and worsening environmental conditions. Both of these factors constitute potential threats to the longer-term competitiveness of the city-region.

In practice, local anti-growth sentiments have been overridden by a combination of central government intervention in the structure planning process and regional policy development. At a local level, however, planning in the city-region is characterised by a political culture that has been reluctant to make explicit a long-term vision of how growth might be accommodated. As a consequence, it has proved difficult to develop strategic responses to the growth management challenges that the city-region faces, and to plan for the level of infrastructure investment required to sustain economic competitiveness in the future.

These difficulties are reinforced by the fragmented structure of local governance in the city-region. The city-regional tier of government was a victim of the mid-1990s local government reform in this area, as in other city-regions. Preparation of strategic planning and transport policy relies on collaboration and consensus building between the four separate authorities. As already discussed, Bristol City itself is severely under-bounded in administrative terms, and lacks control over areas of potential expansion in housing and employment terms beyond the existing built-up area, reinforcing the importance of inter-authority collaboration in relation to planning. Local authority perspectives in the planning process, however, are dominated by a process of defensive competition, attempting to shift housing growth pressures elsewhere and resist further urban encroachment. Local governance has been further complicated by the creation of an increasing number of separate local partnerships involved in local economic development, urban regeneration, housing and other fields (see Chapter 7). Local Strategic Partnerships are also developing, and may in the future begin to engage in serious negotiation and compromise over strategic growth issues. However, the current institutional arrangements, as well as the absence of a strong city-region perspective in governance terms, are inadequate for dealing with issues of territorial interdependence and resolving sensitive questions of growth and its distribution.

Current planning policy at national and local level is putting much stronger emphasis on the recycling of brownfield land within urban areas for new housing development. In line with the recommendations of Lord Rogers' Urban Task Force and new planning policy guidance on housing (Urban Task Force, 1999; DETR, 2000b), Urban Capacity Studies have been carried out, with the aim of identifying the scope for new housing development within urban areas in the sub-region. In the light of these, it is intended that the future pattern of new housing development will shift away from a predominantly suburban pattern, with a significantly higher proportion taking the form of high-density urban schemes within the built-up area of Bristol. To the extent that this policy can be realised in market terms, this implies some reinforcement of trends to decentralisation of employment and re-centralisation of housing, thereby modifying further the traditional model of urban structure in the city-region.

Conclusion

Economic restructuring, combined with a specific set of local government arrangements and local political attitudes to development and planning regulation in the Bristol city-region has led, since the 1970s, to a significant re-shaping of the economic geography of the city-region. The Bristol north fringe has attracted an enormous amount of private investment and has been one of the fastest growing areas in the country in terms of jobs and population. Moreover, it has established itself as an attractive location for companies in dynamic 'knowledge industries' and contributed to the buoyancy of the wider city-region and regional economy in the face of structural economic change. This has been accompanied by some reorientation in the role and function of the city centre, including some threat to the traditional employment role of the CBD. This pattern of development has, however, also been associated with growing spatial inequalities in the wider city-region and environmental threats in the form of high levels of traffic growth and growing levels of traffic congestion.

To what extent is the Bristol example typical of changing urban form more generally? Broader analyses of the geography of employment change in the British urban system would suggest it is not entirely atypical. As the analysis in Breheny (1999, p 210) indicates, the label 'counter-urbanisation' may be misleading in the context of employment. Many of the non-urban districts with high levels of employment growth in the south of England are at least in part suburban areas of larger cities. Edge-of-city growth is clearly not the only form of employment dispersal taking place, but it may form a significant component of the apparent decentralisation of jobs. As Breheny (1999) also notes, boundaries can also be misleading in the other direction. For example, Leeds, apparently the most successful of the UK's larger cities in employment terms, is a particularly generously bounded city, and most growth has taken place in the outer part of the conurbation. In the Bristol case, however, local authority boundaries, coupled with weak strategic planning and the divergence of local political and policy stances towards development and its regulation, may have resulted in a more exaggerated pattern of edge-of-city growth than elsewhere.

A 'laissez-faire' attitude in planning terms in the 1980s and early 1990s also facilitated a relatively dispersed, highly car-dependent form of development. There was little attempt to effectively shape the pattern of development in the Bristol north fringe, or manage its integration with transport infrastructure, in a context where central government policy advocated deregulation in planning terms and promoted the privatisation of public transport. Similar outcomes are also evident elsewhere across the UK, including the M4 corridor running westward out of London (Sudjec, 1992), central Scotland (Bramley, 1999) and the North East (Byrne, 2001). The specific development and policy processes leading to these development outcomes may vary from city to city. However, more general comment on changing urban form (for example, Sudjec, 1992), together with casual observation, would suggest that the character of development in the Bristol north fringe is not unusual.

In Bristol, however, the past failures of the planning system to properly manage growth have taken on added significance in the context of debates about future growth and its management. The perceived negative impacts of the kind of development that has taken place in the north fringe have reinforced local political and popular opposition to further development, contributing to the current difficulties of 'short-termism' and making long-term strategy explicit.

Local policy in the Bristol city-region now recognises the need to 'restructure' the edge-of-city growth that has taken place, through promoting a greater mix of uses and more integrated and compact forms of development, together with significant improvements in public transport infrastructure (South Gloucestershire Council, 2000). The implementation difficulties of such a strategy should not, however, be underestimated given the pattern of development that has emerged since the 1970s. The strategy also sits uncomfortably with the resistance locally to continued development, given that infrastructure investment is increasingly dependent on private sector contributions in the context of major development.

Ongoing controversy in the Bristol city-region about development trajectories and the management of growth pressures is also symptomatic of wider problems of governance at city-region level. Institutional fragmentation and limited strategic capacity at the city-region scale has been recognised as a more general problem in UK cities (CCG, 1999; Robson et al, 2000b). There is also evidence that some city-regions have managed to establish effective inter-authority arrangements, with the capacity to build consensus about how economic growth and environmental priorities may be reconciled. For example, Wenban-Smith (2002) describing Birmingham, and Kumar and Paddison (2000) describing Glasgow, provide positive evaluations of the operation of joint working in relation to strategic planning for the city-region. What may be different in these city-regions in comparison with Bristol, however, is the scope for building consensus around the issue of economic regeneration in regions that have experienced significant economic decline. In growth areas, where planning is often characterised by strongly divergent priorities of economic development versus environmental protection and inter-authority conflict, effective collaboration and consensus may be more difficult to achieve. Added to this, metropolitan areas at least have some legacy of sub-regional working in the past, while cities like Bristol generally lack any history of strong sub-regional collaboration. In other words, there may be systematic differences between the inherent institutional capacity of growth areas as against areas with a history of decline, and between those with a legacy of collaborative working and those without.

In cities like Bristol, however, the need for a positive accommodation of growth pressures, and concerted efforts to overcome the infrastructure deficits and growing spatial inequalities generated in the past, tends to reinforce arguments for a strengthening of arrangements for planning at the city-region scale. It also implies a reversal of the pattern of institutional fragmentation where the different sectors of economic development, housing and urban regeneration are discussed in separate arenas, involving different political and other institutional actors.

Current developments are somewhat contradictory in this context. On the one hand, Local Strategic Partnerships offer the prospect of more coherent policy development and delivery, although with the risk that local partnerships will focus inwards on single local authority districts rather than out to the city-region. Reforms to the planning system are also in prospect (DTLR, 2001a; ODPM, 2003b), which seek to simplify and speed up the operation of planning. Structure plans are to be abolished and regional assemblies will produce statutory Regional Spatial Strategies, supplemented where necessary by sub-regional policy frameworks. The Bristol city-region has been identified as an area where a sub-regional framework will be developed as part of the South West Regional Spatial Strategy, and a sub-regional partnership comprising local government leaders and executive members, together with economic, social and environmental partners, is being established. Their role will be to advise the regional assembly on a strategic vision and policy framework for the city-region. The key difference to the previous joint strategic planning arrangements is that 'partners' from outside of local government will now be formally involved in sub-regional policy development, but ultimate decisions will lie with the Secretary of State, who will approve the new Regional Spatial Strategies. In a separate initiative the West of England Strategic Partnership, a sub-regional economic partnership recognised by the Regional Development Agency, is also developing a sub-regional vision and strategy, driven by business concerns to sustain the long-term competitiveness of the city-region and overcome the serious infrastructure deficit.

Policy at national level (ODPM, 2003a) is also now proposing to tackle what is seen as growing under-supply of housing in many parts of the country and consequent problems of affordability, with particular emphasis on four major growth areas in the South East. A supplementary report on the South West region notes the strong population growth pressures in the region, the need to meet targets for new housing and to plan for growth in the main towns and cities, although it falls short of specifying how this should be achieved in spatial terms. Therefore, at national, regional and sub-regional levels, discussions are taking place that potentially raise the stakes in the discourse about the future of the city-region, and may provoke a more constructive debate about the longer-term future. It remains to be seen whether a stronger national policy steer concerning growth and development, together with institutional development at the regional and sub-regional level, will mark a turning point in the spatial management of the Bristol city-region.

4

City of money?

Shaun French and Andrew Leyshon

Introduction

This chapter is concerned with the geographical impacts of the retail financial services industry. In particular, it seeks to document the urban impacts of financial services through a case study of the city of Bristol, paying close attention to the issues of competitiveness and social cohesion. There has been major growth in the financial services sector in the Bristol city-region since the early 1970s. This has reflected a combination of the relocation of London-based banks and insurance companies, together with subsequent rapid growth and diversification in financial services in the 1980s in the context of deregulation, and continuing expansion in these large local employers (Boddy et al, 1986). However, since the early 1990s the retail financial services sector in the UK has been characterised by large-scale restructuring. Right across the industry, new practices and procedures have gradually been put in place which have transformed the traditional organisational and competitive logic of financial services, including the introduction of telephone-based service channels, centralisation of processing, cross-selling, credit scoring, third-party administration, and the establishment of Internet-based operations. Given the scale of financial services employment locally, the potential impacts of these changes for Bristol are considerable.

The purpose of the Bristol city financial services study was to explore the implications of this radical industrial transformation for the Bristol city-region as a whole. In this chapter, we seek to report on some of the findings of the study conducted during the period 1998 through to spring 2001. We begin by providing a brief review of some of the changes that have taken place in the industry over the last three decades, focusing on the restructuring that has characterised the period from the beginning of the 1990s through to the present day. This will provide important background to the next section of this chapter, in which, by drawing on desk-based research and survey interviews, we attempt to assess how well Bristol has fared in the face of such competitive restructuring. We attempt to do so, first, by analysing employment data for Bristol and the other UK regional financial centres. A key finding of this analysis is that, in comparison to other centres, Bristol has performed relatively poorly over the last decade. In trying to explain this turn of events, the chapter then proceeds to look in more detail at Bristol's competitiveness through the prism of three key indicators. First, we seek to assess how Bristol has fared in the face of competitive restructuring, including the introduction of new telephone-based delivery systems, in the financial services industry. Second, we look at Bristol's role as a regional service centre, particularly for commercial and corporate financial services. Third, we attempt to measure Bristol's competitiveness in terms of its success in adapting to, and taking advantage of new markets, products and ways of doing business. In the fourth part of the chapter, we look at the issue of social cohesion and, in particular, seek to explore the relationship between the concept of social cohesion, competitiveness and the financial services sector in Bristol. The final part of the chapter is given over to a discussion of the ways in which this study can help to inform policy agendas.

The changing face of retail financial services in the UK

Before we outline the changing fortunes of Bristol's financial services sector, we need first to place these changes within the context of the wider reorganisation of the retail financial services industry within the UK since the mid-1980s. This will help to identify the distinctive features of the development of financial services within the Bristol city-region.

Up until the 1970s, the retail financial services industry grew steadily if, symptomatically, in a rather unremarkable manner. This growth was, for the most part, in line with broader social changes, such as the growth of managerial and professional employment, the increase in home ownership and, most significantly, the shift towards the payment of salaries and wages in the form of bank-to-bank transfers rather than in cash for reasons of efficiency and security.

Such transfers were made possible by the industry's enthusiastic and early adoption of information technology from the 1950s onwards, which was largely used to speed-up the 'back office' activities of account processing and settlement (Leyshon and Pollard, 2000). As these technologies were introduced, many firms began to centralise their back-office functions within new divisions. Initially, due to their novelty and relative instability, such facilities were located close to corporate headquarters, which usually meant being located in London. However, as these technologies became increasingly commonplace and routine, several financial services firms took the opportunity to relocate these large operations out of London to locations where property and labour costs were cheaper. A wave of financial office decentralisations began in the 1970s, which initially benefited cities in the South East region – such as Reading and Brighton, for example – but then later more distant locations within the South West, such as Bournemouth, Swindon and Bristol (see the discussion later in this chapter).

This period of relative stability ended in the 1980s when the financial services industry underwent an unprecedented process of change and rupture, the catalyst for which was a sea change in the regulatory framework that controlled the activities of financial services. In particular, from the mid-1980s onwards, the old system of structural regulation was dismantled on the grounds that it discouraged competition and failed to properly serve the consumer. In its place, a new system of 'prudential' regulation was installed, one that would allow firms from different parts of the financial services market to directly compete with one another, bringing about efficiency gains, and which would guard against systemic risk by more actively policing the activities of financial services firms, requiring such firms to more actively demonstrate compliance with regulations (Gardener and Molyneux, 1990). Following legislation enacted in 1986, which included both the Finance Services Act and the Building Societies Act, banks, building societies, insurance companies and other firms that had previously dutifully ploughed their own furrows in strictly demarcated product areas, were free to move into each other's markets.

The increase in competition within financial markets that ensued produced a number of significant outcomes. These included an increase in the number of financial products available, as firms attempted to distinguish themselves from their competitors through new product offerings. In addition, the industry became more inclusive, as both re-regulation and competition swept away the queues and rationing that was a by-product of structural regulation, resulting in more people being able to obtain credit and debt products than was previously the case. Finally, and significantly, the financial services industry became a significant source of new employment as the number of people employed in the financial services industry increased significantly over the period (Leyshon et al, 1989).

However, in the early 1990s, this period of rapid growth ended, as the financial economy, and the economy in general, 'overheated'. As interest rates began to rise to historically new levels at the end of the 1980s, the retail financial services sector underwent a period of retrenchment. This brought about significant changes in both the organisation of firms and in the regulatory framework that surrounded the industry.

The high rates of interest succeeded in slowing inflation, but also introduced a debt crisis within the UK financial services sector, as house prices plummeted, the economy slowed and levels of unemployment increased, including levels of unemployment within the financial services sector (Leyshon and Thrift, 1997). Further problems for the sector were revealed when charges of 'mis-selling' were directed at the industry, particularly in the area of private pensions. Under pressure to make sales targets and increase commissions, it was revealed that a number of representatives of retail financial services firms had sold products to customers that either they did not need or which significantly financially disadvantaged them.

As a result of these outcomes, the financial services industry underwent significant changes during the 1990s. For their part, financial services companies responded to their emerging debt-related difficulties by revamping their systems of risk assessment and risk management. Firms sought to discriminate more clearly between 'good' and 'bad' customers and to identify the potential value of customers to overall profitability. This led to the centralisation of credit control and risk assessment (Leyshon and Thrift, 1999), and the rise of new distribution networks for selling financial services, such as telephone (and later Internet) banking, enabled banks and other financial services to reconsider the role of their branch networks. Around 20% of bank and building society branches were closed in the early 1990s, many of them in the poorest or most remote locations (Leyshon and Thrift, 1997). This closure wave was accompanied by a change in employment patterns as a wave of middle managers (many of them former bank managers) were made redundant. At the same time, financial services firms began to recruit much less expensive employees to work in the call-centre operations that at first supplemented, but then increasingly came to replace, activities formerly performed within branches (Richardson et al, 2000).

Leading retail financial services firms were encouraged to downgrade the role of their branch networks as a way of both tightening control over credit and risk and to reduce costs; branches being the main source of operational costs. Telephone banking and the utilisation of credit scoring systems became new core competencies within the financial services industry. This made it possible for non-financial services firms – such as Marks & Spencer, Virgin, Kwik Fit, for example – to capture significant shares of certain retail financial markets on the back

of a strong brand, and to cherry-pick the most profitable part of those markets. Traditional financial service firms responded in various ways to such pressures. One strategy has involved developing Internet-based divisions – such as Intelligent Finance (Halifax), Egg (Prudential) and Smile (Co-operative Bank), for example – which seek to drive costs down further in the search for more lucrative customers. Another strategy has seen some firms attempt to break into the so-called sub-prime market – that is, the lower end of the market that in the past has been dominated by a set of niche, door-to-door providers (see Leyshon et al, 2004: forthcoming). They have done this by attempting to use more advanced credit scoring systems to skim off the less risky parts of this inherently risky market (Burton et al, 2003).

Bristol and the new competition: sustaining success?

As indicated earlier in this chapter, the current high profile of financial services within the Bristol-city region is in large part a legacy of changes that took place in the 1970s and 1980s. During this period, Bristol was one of a number of cities to benefit from the relocation of large financial services providers out of the City of London and the expansion of the industry as a whole. It was a city at the forefront of what Leyshon et al (1989) described – based on an analysis of key indicators of the relative importance of a financial centre – as the re-emergence of provincial financial centres. In particular, Leyshon et al identified five indicators, three of which can be considered primary measures of the importance of a financial centre:

1. the number of *key financial functions* located in a city;
2. the importance of *finance-related occupations* in relation to the overall occupation structure;
3. the total number of people *employed* locally within the financial services sector.

Of these three, employment data is the most regularly and readily available. Following Leyshon et al (1989), a good place to begin examining Bristol's success since the early 1990s is, therefore, to look at the geography of financial services employment during the 1990s.

However, as a precursor to analysing the geography of financial services employment, there is a need to make clear what it is we mean by financial services. Table 4.1 provides a working definition based on national Standard Industrial Classification (SIC) data of what we broadly define, in the context of this chapter and the study as a whole, as the financial services sector. Standard Industrial Classifications form the building blocks upon which government Census data on business activity is collected and collated by the Office for National Statistics. Our definition of financial services not only includes those activities which are grouped under the heading of Financial Intermediation in the SIC,

- monetary intermediation (such as banks and building societies);
- other financial intermediation (such as credit card and Unit Trust companies);
- auxiliary to financial intermediation (such as stock broking);
- insurance and pension funding (such as life and general insurance);
- auxiliary to insurance and pension funding (such as insurance agents and brokers).

but also two additional activities which are classified under the SIC as business activities:

- legal activities;
- accountancy.

Despite not being pure forms of financial intermediation, much of the commercial business conducted by accountancy and legal firms complements and strongly overlaps with the services offered by other financial services companies. Indeed, for much financial business, both commercial and retail, the services of accountancy and legal practices are integral, as was dramatically illustrated in the case of the Enron scandal in the US. The boundary between those firms operating in the legal and accountancy world and those in the wider financial services industry has also become increasingly blurred as firms seek to diversify their activities. To reflect this we have opted for the broader definition of financial services detailed in Table 4.1.

On the basis of this broad definition, Tables 4.2 and 4.3 rank the 10 travel-to-work areas with the highest

number of full-time equivalent financial services employees for the years 1991, 1993, 1995 and 1995/96, 1998 and 2000/01 respectively. The presentation of data in two distinct time periods reflects changes in employment survey methodologies and, in particular, the decision by the Office for National Statistics to replace the Annual Employment Survey with the Annual Business Inquiry in the mid-1990s, thus problematising longitudinal comparison. Bearing this and the limitations of an analysis at the travel-to-work area scale in mind, both Tables 4.2 and 4.3 clearly highlight the continued pre-eminence of London[9]. The capital remains without doubt the largest concentration of financial services activity within the country. Further, the figures suggest that following a slight contraction of −2.2% between 1991 and 1995 (Table 4.2), in line with the national trend, employment in the capital has grown significantly in the latter part of the decade with a 14.8% increase between 1995/96 and 2000/01.

Turning to the case of Bristol we see that, in spite of a brief rebound in 1995/96 (Table 4.3), the position of the city has slipped from fifth largest financial centre at the beginning of the 1990s to that of sixth in 2000/01. Although, for the reasons just discussed, caution has to be exercised when comparing data from 1991, the numbers employed in financial services in Bristol have stayed close to the 30,000 mark throughout the decade. During the early part of the 1990s employment in Bristol grew by 1.7%, in contrast to a decline of −2.2% in London and −2.8% nationally during the same period (Table 4.2). However, Table 4.2 also shows that, with the notable exception of Manchester and Liverpool, Bristol's competitors enjoyed much stronger growth rates

---

[9] Following Leyshon et al (1989), a similar analysis has been conducted elsewhere using data at the scale of local authority districts. Focus on the urban core and utilisation of a narrow definition of financial services leaves Bristol ranked a better fourth behind London, Edinburgh and Birmingham – reflecting the concentration of large financial services employers in the centre of the city (Bailey and French, 2003: forthcoming). Despite moving Bristol up the rankings, analysis at this scale shows that employment levels were static from 1991/93 to 1998/2000 in contrast, for example, to an increase of 35% in the case of Glasgow and 24% for Edinburgh over the same period (see Bailey and French, 2003: forthcoming).

Table 4.1: Defining financial services

Broad category	Sub-components	SIC no	SIC activity description (1992)
Financial services	A. Monetary intermediation	6511	Central banking
		6512	Other monetary intermediation: • banks • building societies
	B. Other financial intermediation	6521	Financial leasing
		6522	Other credit granting: • credit granting by non-deposit taking finance houses and other specialist consumer credit grantors • factoring • activities of mortgage finance companies • other credit granting
		6523	Other financial intermediation: • investment trusts • unit and property trusts • security dealing • venture and development capital
	C. Auxiliary to financial intermediation	6711	Administration of financial markets
		6712	Security broking and fund management: • stockbroking
		6713	Other auxiliary activities
	D. Insurance and pension funding	6601	Life insurance
		6602	Pension funding
		6603	Non-life insurance
	E. Auxiliary to insurance and pension funding	6720	Auxiliary to insurance and pension funding: • insurance agents and brokers • insurance risk and damage evaluators
	F. Legal activities	7411	Legal activities
	G. Accountancy	7412	Accounting, book-keeping and auditing activities; tax consultancy

from 1991-95. Looking at Table 4.3, we see that Bristol's relatively poor performance compared to its competitor financial centres continued in the latter part of the 1990s. In contrast to very strong rates of employment growth for Manchester (17%), Glasgow (25.1%) and Edinburgh (34.6%), for example, employment in Bristol actually declined by −9.3% between 1995/96 and 2000/01 (Table 4.3). Further analysis of the data reveals that much of the fall in employment levels has occurred since 1999 and, most particularly, since 2000 (Figure 4.1). While it is too early to determine whether the recent decline in numbers employed in the Bristol travel-to-work area

represents a short-term dip, similar to that of 1993 and 1998, or the beginnings of a longer-term reversal, what Figure 4.1 clearly shows is the emergence of a disparity between Bristol's relatively static performance and the upward trajectory of its major competitors. Whereas Edinburgh, for example, began the 1990s in a comparative position to Bristol, it ended the decade challenging for the position of the second largest centre in the UK for financial services, broadly defined, and the largest travel-to-work area outside of London for financial services employment, excluding accountancy and legal services. Similarly, growth in financial services

Table 4.2: Top 10 financial centres ranked by employment (1991-95)

Rank	1991[a] TTWA[b]	FTE[c]	1993[a] TTWA[b]	FTE[c]	1995[a] TTWA[b]	FTE[c]	1991-95 Absolute	%
1	London	375,729	London	354,135	London	367,641	−8,088	−2.2
2	Manchester	43,486	Manchester	39,858	Birmingham	41,441	2,556	6.6
3	Birmingham	38,885	Birmingham	39,791	Manchester	40,118	−3,368	−7.7
4	Edinburgh	32,058	Edinburgh	30,943	Edinburgh	34,086	2,029	6.3
5	Bristol	30,773	Glasgow	30,663	Glasgow	31,460	2,153	7.3
6	Glasgow	29,307	Bristol	27,538	Bristol	31,258	525	1.7
7	Heathrow	26,725	Liverpool	25,433	Leeds	26,217	1,854	7.6
8	Liverpool	26,311	Heathrow	23,675	Heathrow	24,479	−2,246	−8.4
9	Leeds	24,363	Leeds	22,853	Liverpool	23,481	−2,830	−10.8
10	Southend	17,219	Crawley	15,242	Crawley	17,377	950	5.8
Britain		1,269,186		1,207,560		1,233,988	−35,198	−2.8

Notes:
[a] Annual employment survey employee analysis.
[b] Travel-to-work area (1984).
[c] Full-time equivalent employment (full-time employees plus half part-time employees).

▓ Pre-eminent centre

▒ Regional centre

Table 4.3: Top 10 financial centres ranked by employment (1995-2001)[a]

Rank	1995/96[b] TTWA[d]	FTE[e]	1998[c] TTWA[d]	FTE[e]	2000/01[c] TTWA[d]	FTE[e]	1991-95-2000/01 Absolute	%
1	London	393,310	London	406,092	London	451,410	58,100	14.8
2	Birmingham	44,213	Birmingham	45,927	Manchester	48,566	7,044	17.0
3	Manchester	41,523	Manchester	44,335	Birmingham	45,851	1,637	3.7
4	Edinburgh	30,059	Edinburgh	30,054	Edinburgh	44,500	11,441	34.6
5	Bristol	32,309	Glasgow	32,054	Glasgow	39,189	7,865	25.1
6	Glasgow	29,307	Leeds	29,511	Bristol	29,315	−2,995	−9.3
7	Leeds	26,655	Bristol	29,394	Heathrow	28,691	3,478	13.8
8	Heathrow	25,213	Heathrow	29,152	Leeds	28,537	1,882	7.1
9	Liverpool	23,399	Liverpool	21,042	Liverpool	24,804	1,405	6.0
10	Crawley	17,413	Norwich	17,989	Brighton	17,648	6,439	57.5
Britain		1,270,768		1,337,397		1,389,568	118,801	9.3

Notes:
[a] Figures have been averaged for 1995/96 and 2000/01 to minimise sampling errors.
[b] Annual employment survey rescaled employee analysis.
[c] Annual business inquiry employee analysis.
[d] Travel-to-work area (1984).
[e] Full-time equivalent employment (full-time employees plus half part-time employees).

▓ Pre-eminent centre

▒ Regional centre

employment in Leeds has brought the city on a par with Bristol (Figure 4.1).

A breakdown of financial services employment in Bristol (Table 4.4) reveals that there have been significant variations in the performance of different sub-sectors during the late 1990s. Bristol has performed particularly poorly in the monetary intermediation, insurance and pensions, and activities auxiliary to insurance sub-sectors. On the other hand, there has been strong growth in the auxiliary to financial intermediation, accountancy and legal services areas. Despite a fall in the numbers employed, Bristol continues to be characterised by an above-average concentration of activity in the monetary intermediation, and most especially

Figure 4.1: Comparison of the fortunes of the major regional financial centres in the UK

a) Financial services – broad definition (includes accountancy and legal services)

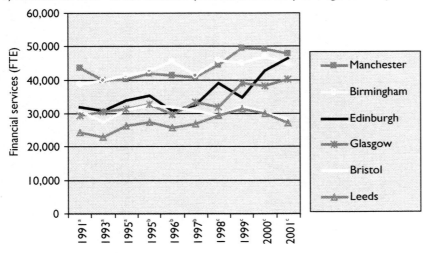

b) Financial services – narrow definition (excludes accountancy and legal services)

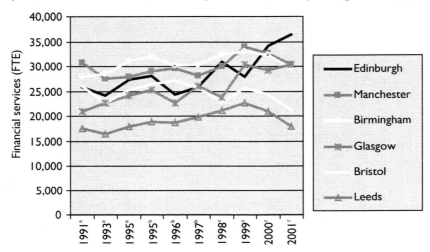

Notes:
[a] Annual Employment Survey employee analysis.
[b] Annual Employment Survey rescaled employee analysis.
[c] Annual Business Inquiry employee analysis.

insurance and pensions, and auxiliary to insurance sub-sectors (see Figure 4.2). Location quotients for the other sub-sectors suggest that Bristol does not have an extraordinary specialisation in these areas. In contrast to more larger financial centres such as the City of London and Edinburgh, Bristol's competitiveness in financial services is much more skewed to particular sectors, namely banking, mortgage provision, insurance and insurance broking.

During the 1970s and 1980s, the headquarter functions of London Life, Phoenix Life (now subsumed in the Royal Sun Alliance Group), Sun Life and London Life insurance companies all relocated from the London area to Bristol (Boddy et al, 1986). In the mid-1970s one of the country's largest legal expenses insurer, DAS, was also established. Bristol is also the home of the Merchant & Investors insurance company. In the 1990s NatWest established its life assurance subsidiary, NatWest Life, in the city while Direct Line has set up a large operation in the city centre. As well as insurance companies, Bristol boasts the headquarters of two major national insurance brokers, Hill House

Figure 4.2: Location quotients for selected financial centres (2000)

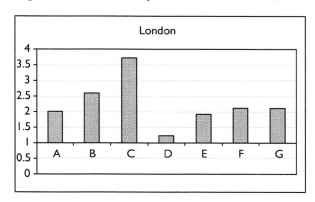

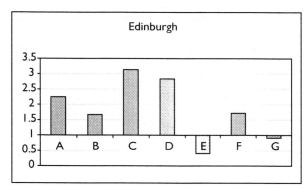

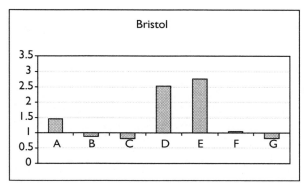

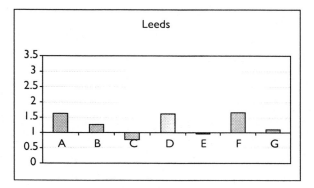

Key: See Table 4.1 for sectoral definitions.

Table 4.4: Sub-components of financial services sector in Bristol

| | Bristol (1984 TTWA) | | | |
| | 1995/96[a] | 2000/01[b] | 1995/96-2000/01 | |
Financial services	FTE	FTE	Absolute	%
Monetary intermediation	10,723	8,532	−2,191	−20.4
Other financial intermediation	1,356	1,381	25	1.8
Auxiliary to financial intermediation	390	940	550	141.3
Insurance and pensions	8,773	7,716	−1,057	−12.0
Auxiliary to insurance	5,532	4,232	−1,300	−23.5
Legal services	3,348	3,977	629	18.8
Accountancy	2,188	2,536	349	15.9
Total	32,309	29,315	−2,995	−9.3

Hammond and NatWest Insurance Services. Other insurance companies with a significant local presence include Cornhill and CGNU. Again, despite recent reversals in the numbers employed in insurance and insurance broking, these sectors still constituted over 40% of financial services employment in Bristol in 2000/01. Further, the concentration of life assurance activity in the Bristol city-region has led the Department of Trade and Industry to identify life assurance as a local 'high-point' industry in its recent report on clusters in the UK (DTI, 2001). In terms of the second most significant concentration of activity, that of banking and mortgage provision, Bristol is the home of Lloyds TSB's retail banking headquarters and the headquarters of Bristol & West mortgage bank. In addition, the other big three high street banks – HSBC, Barclays and NatWest – all have significant offices in the city.

Having looked at the broad picture in terms of levels of employment, we will now attempt to take a closer look at how Bristol has fared in the light of the emerging new competition in financial services described earlier. The survey findings discussed here are drawn from desk-based research and interviews conducted during the main period of the Bristol city financial services study from 1998 through to the end of 2000. Since then, employment data for the years 2000 and 2001 has become available and is incorporated in what follows. Explanations of the role and importance of financial centres have stressed many different factors. In attempting to synthesise these factors into a more general theoretical framework, Parr and Budd (2000) argue that financial centres can be understood in terms of trade-offs between three groups of factors. These are: the nature of demand; internal economies of scale or scope; and external economies of scale, scope and complexity (Bailey and French, 2003: forthcoming). In what follows, the role of internal economies, demand and external economies, together with more socioeconomic factors such as institutional thickness, will be explored through an analysis of three key measures of Bristol's competitiveness. First, we look at the impact of competitive restructuring in terms of market consolidation; second, the application of information technology (IT) and use of call centres; third, the role of Bristol as a centre for servicing regional demand for financial services and, fourth, evidence of innovation and learning in Bristol.

Competitive restructuring

Market consolidation

One of the most visible aspects of restructuring has been an intensification of merger and acquisition activities, particularly in the insurance, mortgage and banking sectors. In response to more competitive and internationalised markets, and under the influence of investors and analysts in the City of London, there has been a wave of mergers and acquisitions as firms seek to build critical mass, tap into new markets, diversify their revenue streams and, crucially, to cut costs. Much of these deals have involved organisations with significant operations in Bristol. In the banking sector, examples include the merger in 1995 of Lloyds and TSB, the takeover of NatWest by the Royal Bank of Scotland, Barclays' purchase of the Woolwich, and the acquisition of Midland Bank by the HSBC group. Also of significance has been Bank of Ireland's acquisition of Bristol & West, Cheltenham & Gloucester and Scottish Widows becoming part of Lloyds TSB group, and Halifax's acquisition of the Bristol-based life and pensions provider Clerical Medical, prior to Halifax's subsequent merger with the Bank of Scotland. Important deals in the insurance sector include the merger of Royal Insurance and Sun Alliance to create Royal Sun Alliance, Commercial Union and General Accident's merger to become CGU, and CGU's subsequent merger with Norwich Union (the owner of the Bristol insurance broker Hill House Hammond) to create CGNU. Finally, in the late 1990s Sun Life was acquired by the AXA group, their business was then merged with that of AXA Equity & Law, and a little further afield Allied Dunbar in Swindon has become part of the Zurich Financial Services group. Numerous less high-profile examples could also be given, but what this list illustrates is the clear significance of the intensification of merger and acquisition activity for Bristol.

How has Bristol fared in the wake of such activity? The research we conducted suggested that on the whole Bristol had fared pretty well. Mergers and acquisitions represent an attractive option for companies and their shareholders because, among other things, they enable firms to cut costs and increase efficiency by getting rid of duplication and rationalising operations. Mergers and acquisitions also provide a window of opportunity for firms to

Table 4.5: The impact on Bristol of selected merger and acquisition deals

Insurance	Estimated employment	
	Pre-deal	Post-deal
Case 1	200[a]	230[a]
Case 2	2,000[a]	2,000[a]
Case 3	2,500[a]	3,000[a]
Banking and mortgages		
Case 1	1,800[b]	1,900[b]
Case 2	2,000-2,500[a]	2,500-3,00[a]

Notes:

[a] Combined employment in Bristol of both firms, before and after merger (not including local employment in mortgage or banking branch network).

[b] Bristol employment in single firm, before and after acquisition by rival.

Source: Authors' interviews and research (1998-2000)

more generally restructure their activities. Now, although nearly all the deals studied involved some element of operational restructuring, office closure, staff relocation and redundancy, the aggregate impact on Bristol in terms of numbers employed and operations carried out in the city appeared to be relatively neutral, even slightly positive. Interviews with senior managers working in the Bristol offices of three of the most significant recent post-merger insurance companies suggested that resultant restructuring had not had a detrimental effect on local levels of employment. Indeed, in one case business restructuring had actually led to an increase in the numbers employed locally, reflecting a decision from now on to source all of the combined life assurance business to Bristol (see Table 4.5). Further, whereas post-merger operational capacity was relatively unchanged in the first case, an important consequence of the second merger was that client services were to be concentrated in only two national operational centres, Bristol and Liverpool, following the closure of the four other pre-merger UK centres. The Bristol centre became responsible for all new life business, as well as the administration of a significant proportion of the existing pre-merger life policies.

Interviews with senior managers in two other companies at the centre of merger and acquisition deals in the banking and mortgage markets in the latter half of the 1990s also suggested that Bristol had not been detrimentally affected by these rounds of restructuring. Indeed, in the second case, Bristol had again actually benefited from such activity. Anecdotal evidence of other acquisitions and mergers at the

time in both these sectors suggested that Bristol also appears to have fared reasonably well.

What explanations were given for Bristol's apparent success in holding onto offices and jobs in the face of intensifying merger and acquisition activity? Interviews with the case study companies suggested that a key factor was sunk costs, both in terms of labour and embedded capital. For instance, when asked to explain the decision to retain operations in Bristol, the divisional manager of one of the newly merged insurance companies stressed:

> "... the numbers of staff ... and the expertise and service etcetera. And also, I mean the, the cost of doing something different. I mean the sort of severance cost if we closed down a site like this would be astronomical, even assuming you could match that skill somewhere else." (Divisional Manager, insurance case 2)

In addition to the critical factor of not wishing to lose skilled and experience staff, interviewees also stressed the significance of owning or leasing local premises as well as legacy computer systems as factors helping to mitigate against relocation. Inertia and the risks involved in establishing a newly consolidated operation in another location were also factors cited which helped to ensure the continuation of existing activity in Bristol[10]. These reflected formal and informal deadlines imposed by regulators, customers and City investors for the delivery of a quick, smooth and cost-effective merger. However, as previously discussed, the most recent data suggests that employment in monetary intermediation and insurance has subsequently fallen. It may be, then, that in conjunction with continued IT-driven restructuring, to which we will turn next, subsequent rounds of organisational restructuring have taken place less inhibited by such frictions. The sunk costs of competing operations in other larger financial centres may have become more significant, for example.

Information technology and call centres

Should Bristol appear to have been, certainly initially, relatively successful in competing with other places

---

[10] Corporate strategy and the terms and politics of specific deals were other factors that helped to determine the outcome of the mergers and acquisitions in question.

and financial centres in terms of the pressures of continuing market consolidation, how well has the city fared in relation to some of the other significant changes affecting the industry? As previously discussed, IT, together with other factors such as regulatory reform, an increase in competition, mis-selling scandals, changes in the way in which consumers wish to buy financial products and wider societal changes have helped to transform the retail financial services market. Information technology has played a critical role in the restructuring of both the distribution, and processing and administration of financial services, allowing increasing centralisation and operational specialisation. The adoption of credit-scoring technologies and the development of purpose-built processing centres, together with the increasing importance of the telephone and the Internet as distribution mediums has led to the functional hollowing out and rationalisation of bank, mortgage and insurance branch networks. Information technology has also allowed the rationalisation and restructuring of head office and large administrative operations in these sectors.

Just as in the case of Leeds, Manchester, Glasgow and other regional centres, the most immediate manifestation of this process of IT-facilitated corporate restructuring has been the emergence in Bristol of a significant number of financial services call centres. Gripaios et al (1999) have estimated there to be as many as 32 call centres in Bristol, at least eight of which were in the financial services sector. Symbolic of this growth in call centre activity was Direct Line's decision to establish its sixth national call centre in Bristol city centre in 1994. However, Direct Line is an exception, in as much as most of the call centre activity that has developed in Bristol has involved organisations with an existing presence in the city establishing in-house centres. The study identified three processes at work. First, a process of organic growth, with call centre activity growing from existing activities in Bristol. This mechanism is particularly strong in the case of the insurance industry, with both insurance companies and brokers reacting to the demand for telephone-based services by establishing their own call centre operations often, certainly initially, in the same building as their existing activities. Second, the effect of organisational embeddedness, whereby the presence of existing operations had a significant pull effect on a firm's subsequent decision to establish a

new call centre in Bristol. Spare capacity in existing offices and local knowledge were particularly important factors. With respect to the latter, knowledge of the local labour market in terms of recruiting both technical and non-technical staff, knowledge of suitable locations, and a positive experience of running a financial services business in the city were stressed to be important criteria by interviewees in the study. In an increasingly fast moving and competitive market, such local knowledge significantly reduced decision times and the risks involved in making location choices. The establishment of call centres in Bristol also provided those organisations with existing concentrations of activity in the city-region, and in particular the banks, with an opportunity to relocate rather than make redundant employees working in other parts of the organisation that were being scaled back. Third, and finally, there was also a geographical dimension underlying such decisions where, for reasons of company strategy or as a consequence of technological constraints, retail financial institutions established call centres in Bristol in order to specifically serve the district or local region.

These findings help to explain Bristol's relative success in competing with other more popular areas for call centre location, such as Strathclyde, Lothian, South Glamorgan and Tyne and Wear (Bristow et al, 2000) and with rival financial centres such as Leeds, Glasgow and Cardiff. More generally, the case of Bristol, when considered in combination with comparative research conducted into the financial services industry in Edinburgh and Glasgow (Bailey and French, 2003: forthcoming), provides evidence to support the assertion by Bristow et al (2000, p 534) that:

> ... although peripheral regions with low-cost advantages are attractive call centre locations other factors such as the need to minimise risk and to stay close to existing premises, allied activity, and suitable concentrations of labour supply exert a significant influence on location decisions.

Bristol's existing concentration of insurance, mortgage and banking activities, along with the local supply of labour, have been key assets to date in the city's competition for call centre work. However, our research also revealed significant problems that were beginning to threaten Bristol's continuing ability to compete for this type of activity. In particular, interviews with financial services managers highlighted serious shortages of staff with telephony and more general administrative skills. Such shortages had led to an increase in wage costs as employers sought to prevent the poaching of staff by other local operations, a problem exacerbated by the high turnover rates characteristic of call centres. In addition to labour market problems, high local concentrations of existing activity were beginning to have a push rather than a pull effect for a number of organisations thinking of further expanding in-house call centre operations. A number of interviewees, for instance, cited a concern with having all their 'eggs in one basket' as an important reason for deciding to locate new operations outside of Bristol. As a consequence companies were already beginning at the time of the study to look further afield for sites for call centre operations, to the advantage of lower cost locations in the region such as Newport and Plymouth.

Increases in the costs of locating and operating in central Bristol have also been a factor behind the decision by a number of other organisations to decentralise clerical and administrative functions, helping to fuel growth on Bristol's edge-city and drawing operations to places such as Clevedon. At the same time as facilitating the relocation of work out of Bristol, continuing developments in IT are also conversely helping to retain work and activities in the city. The adoption of more sophisticated processing, administration and call centre hardware and software, such as voice recognition software for example, has helped to reduce the number of people required to deal with a given volume of business. By so doing, IT can reduce the imperative for a growing business to seek a cheaper location in terms of labour and premises.

Since the time of the study, the threat to back-office and call centre jobs from new, lower-cost locations has taken on an increasingly international dimension. Bearing out the predictions of several interviewees in the course of the study, and of early movers such as AXA Sun Life, the real threat to Bristol's call centre and back-office jobs now no longer seems to be from other locations in the UK, but increasingly from overseas, and in particular locations such as India. As numerous recent newspaper reports have made clear, cities such as Delhi, with access to a large supply of highly educated, motivated and relatively low-cost workers, represent a considerable threat to a large number of financial services jobs in Bristol and other urban centres in the UK (*The Guardian*, 2003; *The Sunday Times*, 2003). In addition to the impact of second and third rounds of organisational restructuring, the recent reduction in the number of banking and insurance jobs may indicate that regional and international relocation of administrative and call centre jobs is already having an impact on employment levels in Bristol.

While not wishing to underestimate the very real threat posed, our research does suggest some grounds for optimism on Bristol's part. Predictions that IT would drive the wholesale relocation of *all* call centre and back-office jobs to low-cost peripheral locations in the UK failed to take fully into account factors such as the desire to minimise and spread risk, and the desire to locate close to existing premises and allied activity. Similar predictions of the wholesale loss of back-office and call centre jobs to India underestimate the significance of such factors. The Bristol study suggests that these factors are particularly important for newer and smaller-scale operations where levels of uncertainty are relatively high and cost benefits in terms of internal economies of scale relatively low. Thus Bristol, in tandem with many other financial centres, may already be facing difficulties in keeping hold of the larger, more mature and higher profile call and back-office centres. It may, however, be in a better position to retain the larger number of smaller centres, certainly in the short to medium term. Furthermore, as discussed earlier, technological developments such as sophisticated voice recognition software may actually reduce the imperative of companies with even large call centre operations to relocate.

Bristol as a regional financial centre

As Parr and Budd (2000) emphasise, demand is an important factor in understanding the geography of financial services. The need for financial services providers to be located within easy access of their markets and clients has played a key role in the development and continued significance of regional financial centres, and this is no less the case for Bristol. Whereas in the past local demand played an important role in the concentration of customer-facing services in regional centres in both the retail and corporate sectors, recent processes of commodification, distanciation and centralisation have weakened the link between demand and location in the case of the retail financial services. In contrast, the greater complexity and heterogeneity of demand for commercial and corporate financial services has ensured the continued importance of close proximity to markets, to the benefit of cities such as Bristol. So, for instance, in the case of commercial insurance, Bristol continues to benefit from the location of the regional and local offices of many insurance brokers and companies, such as Royal Sun Alliance, AIG and Hill House Hammond. The bespoke nature of commercial insurance business, particularly in the case of medium and large commercial risks, continues to place a premium on face-to-face interaction – between insurance companies, brokers and clients – and therefore geographical proximity:

"... there is development in the smaller end of the commercial business through automated systems ... so for shop insurance or very small commercial type risks ... people are trying to develop the systems which means the broker can actually tap it into the screen to get the quote, rather than having to refer to the ... insurer for the quotation.... When it comes to larger commercial risks, I think being local again and having that understanding and working with the customer to try and achieve something for that risk – risk management is still a very much important area of the business." (Area Director, commercial insurer, personal communication)

Similarly, Bristol benefits from local provision of corporate finance services such as venture capital and private equity finance (for example, Icon Corporate Finance and 3i); the regional offices of the 'big four' accountants; stock-broking services; and corporate legal services (for example, those offered by Bristol-based practices Osborne Clarke, with offices in London, Reading and Frankfurt, and Burgess Salmon, also with a London office). Bristol, therefore, is able to offer a breadth of corporate finance expertise. In explaining this breadth of expertise, the study found evidence to support Leyshon et al's (1989, p 188) argument that an important mechanism of provincial financial centre growth has been the "functional take-off of the City [of London]". According to Leyshon et al (1989, p 188), the resultant "scramble [among City firms] for highly valued internationally-oriented

business" following the revitalisation of the City of London in the 1970s and 1980s created new opportunities for regional providers to compete favourably with City firms for smaller domestic clients, both on price and quality of service. When quizzed about the advantages of operating in Bristol, the chief executive of one local stockbroker active in the corporate and institutional market stressed:

"... the fact that we are far enough away from London to be able to establish some independence. The fact that there are good other professional businesses [here] in terms of lawyers, accountants in Bristol. So in terms of flotation work it's possible to do a whole flotation in Bristol, probably for about half the price you would in London."

Furthermore:

"... our competitors in London are either in a global market place ... or else they are putting their best resources behind the larger companies."

Whereas Leyshon et al (1989) identified the concern of City firms with international markets as being a driving force in the 1980s, interviews with firms suggest that Bristol has been slower than its competitors to take advantage of this opportunity. Two factors may help to explain the lag. First, the local market for such services is smaller than in the case of competitor provincial centres such as Leeds. The local director of a venture capital firm stressed, for instance, the "disparity in the number of quoted PLCs [Public Limited Companies]", whereas "the number of quoted PLCs in Yorkshire and Humberside is about 180. Here [Bristol], it is what? It struggles to be 60".

Second, there was a perception that until recently Bristol had been weak in the area of complementary services, particularly accountancy and legal services, critical for this market:

"When I first arrived [in Bristol] ... having worked in Leeds and Newcastle, it felt like Bristol was definitely second league. Definitely, you know, towards the bottom of division one in terms of professional services. That's changed a lot.... Bristol is [now] punching above its weight when it comes to legal services." (Local Director, venture capitalist firm, personal communication)

Evidence for the recent strengthening of such complementary services in the city is also provided by the strong local growth in employment in both accountancy (15.9%) and legal services (18.8%) since 1995/96 (Table 4.4).

Despite evidence to suggest an apparent strengthening of the local professional services and corporate finance sector, ongoing organisational restructuring presents a threat to Bristol's future role as a regional service hub. In particular, the process of 'regionalisation', the rationalisation of operations by concentrating activity within a smaller number of regional capitals, was highlighted by a number of those interviewed as being a particular threat to Bristol's status. As a consequence of regionalisation, Bristol is forced to compete increasingly with regional rivals such as Cardiff, Southampton and Reading for such activities. In such a competitive environment, it was seen to be vital for Bristol to secure its position as *the* regional capital of the South West, "a city which can support a regional effort" (Local Director, venture capital firm).

Innovation and learning

The third way in which Bristol's competitiveness as a financial centre can be measured is in terms of success in adapting to, and taking advantage of, new markets, products and ways of doing business. A key factor in explaining the competitive success of places like the City of London is that such centres provide important environments for innovation and learning, as a consequence of the high local concentration of financial services activity, and the opportunities for networking thus provided. Firms and individuals within such centres are able to take advantage of these resources, so as to be able to enhance their own competitiveness. However, the measurement of levels of innovation and learning poses considerable problems. In the case of Bristol, the study addressed this issue in two ways. First, by seeking to identify new markets or new ways of doing business in which Bristol exhibited particular strengths. One notable success story in this regard has been the growth of a strong local socially responsible or ethical investment sector. Until quite recently regarded by mainstream providers as peripheral, the past few years have witnessed a significant growth in the stature of the UK socially responsible investment (SRI) market. Increasing social and environmental awareness among

consumers, changes in legislation (notably the requirement under the Pension Schemes Amendment Regulations of 1999 for pension funds to disclose the existence or otherwise of social, environmental or ethical investment criteria), and the legitimisation of the institutions and apparatus of SRI (symbolised by FTSE's decision to launch a range of FTSE4Good, SRI indices in July 2001) have helped fuel growth in products, providers and funds. For a number of reasons, Bristol has developed a particular strength in this industry. It reflects the relatively high demand locally for these sorts of services, which in turn reflects and is illustrated by a long-standing interest in environmental and social issues in the city-region (the city is home to The Schumacher Society, The Soil Association and The CREATE Centre, for example). Triodos, the Dutch social bank, has established its UK head office in Bristol, while a significant proportion of the SRI activity of both specialist independent financial adviser Holden Meehan and the stock broking firm Rathbone Neilson are also based in the city. These organisations have played an important role in the development of the industry in the UK, and in so doing have drawn upon, and contributed to, the wider social and environmental institutional fabric in the city and the region[11]. The clustering of providers and allied institutions in Bristol has provided enhanced opportunities for networking and the development and monitoring of knowledge and information, critical to the investment decisions of such companies. For example, the managing director of a local Bristol-based SRI provider stressed the benefits of the geographical proximity of The Soil Association in developing an organic farming investment strategy:

> "We've been able to really develop work into the organic sector, which is very strong now and growing fast, and that has been helped enormously by the fact that we could develop such good links with The Soil Association."

Notwithstanding the general importance of the development of a concentration of activity within a

---

[11] For instance, in recent years Triodos, Rathbone Neilson and Holden Meehan have sponsored the annual Bristol Schumacher Lectures (heralded as Britain's 'premier environmental gathering'), which in 1998 specifically explored the theme of the 'Ecology of Money'.

new and rapidly expanding area of financial services, the growth of Bristol's embryonic SRI cluster must be put into context. Bristol is undoubtedly important in terms of its contribution to the SRI market, particularly with regard to the development of knowledge and practices, and is better placed to take advantage of continuing growth in this market than many of its competitors. The contribution of the handful of providers, in terms of jobs and income, however, remains small in absolute terms. Furthermore, the bulk of SRI funds are managed, as with all investment funds, by institutions in the City of London rather than Bristol. However, by tapping into Bristol's pool of SRI expertise, local institutions in the much larger and more significant banking and life assurance sectors – significant both in terms of jobs and income generation – could potentially gain competitive advantage in the rapidly expanding SRI market place, for example.

Second, the study more generally sought to find evidence of local infrastructure for innovation and learning. In particular, the study sought to find evidence of local networking, in terms of direct production networks between firms in Bristol, and evidence of social networking within the local financial services industry, which is a form of networking which has a more indirect impact on production. Although evidence of both types of networking was found, the intensity and significance of such processes varied considerably across sectors, both between activities and among different communities. For example, in the case of the provision of business services, social networking between law firms, venture capitalists, accountants and the like was of a much more directly productive nature than that in the insurance and banking industries. With the possible exception of local linkages to the direct marketing industry and between insurance brokers and the local offices of direct insurers, social networking in the case of insurance and banking tended to revolve around career opportunities, work-based friendships, professional development and learning.

In terms of the impact that such networking has on the competitiveness of Bristol as a financial centre, our study suggests that directly productive networking is significant in the case of the provision of business services and the SRI sector. Social networking is important in the case of the insurance

industry and the SRI sector. As in the case of processes of market consolidation and other forms of competitive restructuring, the labour market emerged, together with local professional institutions, as the single most important element in promoting local learning and innovation. As well as evidence that the labour market helped to facilitate learning and innovation in the local life marketing and life underwriting professions (French, 2000, 2002)[12], there was also some evidence to show that local contacts made while working in the legal insurance industry had led directly to the establishment of new firms in Bristol. Having said this, it is clear that the infrastructure for learning and innovation is much more fragmented and patchy in Bristol than in the City of London, for example. Although we would argue that by contributing to the strength of the local labour market such processes of networking play an important role in Bristol's financial competitiveness, it may be that other factors such as the cost of labour, the development of IT, and the cost of office space will play a more significant role in determining Bristol's future as a financial centre.

Financial services and social cohesion

Our primary focus in looking at financial services in Bristol has been issues of competition and competitiveness. However, by drawing on this and other research, particularly that on financial exclusion undertaken by researchers in the Personal Finance Research Centre (PFRC) at the University of Bristol, it is possible to explore some of the relationships between the city's continued significance as a financial centre and of its relation to social cohesion.

As discussed in Chapter 6 of this volume, the current interest in social cohesion and allied terms such as social exclusion and social capital tends to belie, particularly within government circles, the very real problems and complexities of such concepts, and their translation into meaningful policy initiatives (see also Kearns and Forrest, 2000; Forrest and Kearns,

---

[12] Thus providing support that Bristol's life assurance sector does in fact exhibit some characteristics that might justify the DTI's categorisation of life assurance activity in the city as a 'cluster' (DTI, 2001).

2001). In attempting to define the term, Kearns and Forrest (2000, pp 996-1002) identify five distinct dimensions that are used in different ways by different actors in different contexts. The first use is to convey a shared sense of morality and a civic culture. The second use is in relation to social order and control. The third revolves around social solidarity and reductions in wealth disparities. The fourth relates to social interaction, social networks and social capital, while the fifth and final use is in conjunction with ideas of place attachment and identity.

What is meant by social cohesion, therefore, differs quite considerably. Nevertheless, a distinguishing feature of its recent popularity within policy debates, from questions of industrial innovation and economic competitiveness to debates concerning social deprivation and exclusion, has been an assumption that social cohesion is "everywhere virtuous and a positive attribute" (Forrest and Kearns, 2001, p 2129). Problems are often framed as a consequence of a lack of social cohesion, whether in terms of morality, social order or networking, with the answer being to promote more socially cohesive neighbourhoods, cities, city-regions or nation states (see, for instance, SEU, 1998). In contrast, academic debate on the issue has highlighted the complexity of the effects of social cohesion. Kearns and Forrest (2000, p 1013) illustrate, for instance, the importance of taking scale into account — whether national/interurban, city/ city-region, or neighbourhood — in order to properly understand the effects of social cohesion, for as they point out, a "city can consist of socially cohesive but increasingly divided neighbourhoods". As these authors make clear, social cohesion is not simply the opposite of social exclusion. It cannot be simply equated with social stability and harmony; rather, social cohesion can be as much equated with issues of conflict and defence as harmony and stability[13].

Bearing these caveats in mind, what can we say about the relationship between the concept of social cohesion and the financial services sector in Bristol? First, we need to differentiate between the role of social cohesion in contributing to the success or

otherwise of Bristol as a financial centre, and the way in which the financial services industry itself contributes to the social cohesiveness of the city of Bristol. In relation to the former, Kearns and Forrest's (2000) fourth dimension of social cohesion — that of social interaction, social networks and social capital — does appear to be of importance in helping to determine Bristol's competitiveness as a financial centre. As discussed earlier, our research into the financial services sector found evidence of networking of various types among various communities and at various scales. In terms of different types of networking, the study provided evidence both of social networks directly helping to facilitate production and of networks, especially among professionals and other workers involved in similar activities, whose impact on production was more indirect.

The significance of these two types of social networking varied in relation to different communities, different activities and different sectors. However, on the whole our study suggests that in the case of Bristol those social networks with a more indirect impact on production — those connected to local labour markets and communities-of-practice — what Storper (1995) has termed 'untraded interdependencies' — seem to be of the most significance. At least part of the reason for this is the profile of the financial services industry in the city, with the bulk of employment in the vertically integrated sectors of retail banking, mortgage lending and life and general insurance. As such, opportunities for the development of local production networks within these sectors are more limited than in the case of investment banking, for example (Eccles and Crane, 1988). This is not to say that production networks do not exist in these industries: evidence of production networks between local law firms specialising in financial services and organisations in these sectors were found, but that they may be of relatively less importance than in other industries.

In the case of both types of network, social cohesion measured in terms of trust, reciprocity, collective norms and other aspects of social capital (Forrest and Kearns, 2001, p 2140) appears overwhelmingly to be of benefit to the economy of the city. For instance, as illustrated earlier in this chapter, there is evidence in the case of the life assurance sector to suggest that both those locally employed in the life marketing and

---

[13] In terms of the role of social cohesion in issues of industrial innovation and competitiveness, this is reflected in the recognition that local and regional business networks can as often hinder as promote competitiveness and innovation (see Grabher, 1993).

in the life underwriting professions have benefited from interaction with colleagues in other firms in the area (French, 2000, 2002). As such the social cohesiveness of certain communities in the financial services industry appears in general terms to be an asset – rather than a deficit – for Bristol (see Grabher, 1993). However, it is extremely difficult to quantify the importance of this type of social cohesion to Bristol's present or future success as a financial centre. While we have argued that such networking is of significance, it is difficult to say precisely how significant. What is clear is that in comparison to the City of London, social networking in Bristol is much more uneven and of a lower density. This is a consequence of the differing types of financial activity in each centre, the difference in size of the two centres, and the City of London's success in securing its place as an international financial centre (Thrift, 1994). This is not to dismiss the importance of local social networking, particularly in respect of certain communities such as SRI and life underwriting, but to be aware that in the case of Bristol, social networking is only one of a number of city assets, albeit one which helps to constitute other assets, determining Bristol's present and future competitiveness as a financial centre.

Discussion of the issue of city assets brings us to a second way in which social cohesion can be seen to be a factor in Bristol's success or otherwise. As well as the social cohesiveness of the local financial services community, in terms of interaction and networking, Bristol's success in attracting and retaining jobs, companies and professionals is also influenced by the cohesiveness, the strength of social solidarity, order, and the civic culture, of the city as a whole. As with all measures of cohesion there is no simple relationship between the degree of social solidarity, social order and the strength of the local civic culture and that of the attractiveness of Bristol. Social cohesion as interpreted here can either act as an asset or a deficit, as a push or pull factor depending on the nature of the cohesiveness and the perceptions of the firm, organisation or individual in question. Mirroring previous research (Boddy et al, 1986), the study found that the perceived attractiveness of Bristol as a place to live and work was considered by many in the industry to be an important asset.

In contrast to the positive effect of such a perception of relative social harmony and of a certain type of civic culture in the area of education, city-wide disparities, particularly between the state and private school systems, emerged as a significant push factor. As is discussed in the chapter on social cohesion (Chapter 6), Bristol's education system exhibits a particularly pronounced polarity. On the one hand, the state-run school system falls below average with respect to many of the national indicators. On the other hand, Bristol has a large number of private schools. The perceived lack of 'good' state schools and the perception that, as a result, interviewees in financial services companies had little option but to educate their children privately, were issues highlighted time and time again as disadvantages of living and working in Bristol, particularly by managers who had recently relocated to work in the city.

Turning, now, to the question of how the financial services industry itself contributes to the social cohesiveness of Bristol, it is clear that as a generator of jobs and of wealth, and to a lesser extent as a provider of local business services, the sector plays an important role in ensuring the prosperity of the Bristol city-region. By so doing, the financial services sector contributes, if not necessarily to social solidarity and harmony, then at the very least to general social order. At the same time the benefits in terms of income, employment and social capital are certainly not evenly distributed. As is the case in other financial centres and in other industries, social conflict and tension can arise from struggles for access to such social and economic assets. In the case of Bristol, two points of social tension can be identified; first, the disparity between the more secure and professionalised financial services occupations and the larger number of less well-paid and, as discussed earlier, increasingly insecure jobs in administration and call centres, for example.

Second, as well as differences between those working in the industry, marked disparities continue to persist between the employed, on the one hand, and, on the other, the unemployed and those at the margins of the world of work. As described in Chapter 6 of this volume, Bristol, despite its prosperity, continues to be marked by areas of high deprivation. Access or rather a lack of access to financial services has been cited specifically as a key contributory factor to such deprivation and social exclusion. On the back of the publication of the neighbourhood renewal report (SEU, 1998), the government established two policy action teams (PATs) to address the issues of access to personal financial services and to credit for small businesses in deprived areas (HM Treasury, 1999a, 1999b). Significantly, Bristol has featured prominently in the follow-up work to the two PAT reports, both in terms of local access to small business credit (Bank of England, 2000) and, most particularly, to personal financial services (Collard et al, 2001).

Despite the presence of a large number of financial services providers, particular areas of Bristol appear to be significantly affected by problems of financial exclusion. Whereas branches of Coutts and Lloyds TSB's private banking arm serve the wealthier residents and areas of the city, people living in inner-city Barton Hill and other deprived wards often face real problems in accessing such basic services as bank and savings accounts (Collard et al, 2001). A comprehensive study of the problem of financial exclusion in Barton Hill found that despite "being geographically close to the city centre", and thus the headquarters of such institutions as Lloyds TSB and Bristol & West, as many as four out of ten people in Barton Hill were either on the margins or completely excluded from the mainstream financial services market (Collard et al, 2001, p 4). The researchers found that the locality was marked by a "widespread mistrust of financial services providers and a belief that financial services are not for the poor" (2001, p 3). Although processes of financial exclusion are complex, at least part of the problem has to do with the competitive strategies, such as branch closure and credit scoring, adopted by banks and the like in the light of the current competitive environment.

Thus, as well as contributing to social stability by generating jobs and wealth, there is much evidence to suggest that banks, insurance companies and so on are also playing a not insignificant role in fuelling social fragmentation and exclusion in Bristol, as in other cities. Responding to public concern and government pressure, financial services providers, and banks in particular, have become involved in a range of initiatives aimed at addressing this problem at the national and local level. In the case of Barton Hill, representatives of several of the high-street banks have not only been involved in the community

consultation process, but also in ongoing work with the city council, local residents and actors from Bristol's social economy sector in looking at concrete ways in which to address the needs identified by Collard et al (2001). In their report, Collard et al (2001) identify particular demand for bank accounts and savings products, as well as a more general problem with financial literacy. In conclusion, they stress the need for a partnership approach between local organisations and national financial services providers (such as Lloyds TSB's partnership with the Portsmouth Area Regeneration Trust through which the bank provided resources and expertise) so as to be able to build upon and meet gaps in existing provision for the financially excluded in Bristol[14].

As well as personal financial services, the banks have also been involved in initiatives to address the problem of access to finance for small businesses in deprived neighbourhoods (Bank of England, 2000). In the case of Bristol, Lloyds TSB, Bristol & West and the city council have, for instance, provided funding for Bristol Enterprise Development Fund (BEDF). Although BEDF is small, the organisation provides an opportunity for people who would otherwise find it difficult or near impossible to access small business start-up or development loans. In addition to these sorts of partnership schemes, particular organisations in Bristol can also be seen to be addressing problems of social exclusion and division through their adoption of socially responsible lending strategies. By taking into account criteria such as social and environmental sustainability, one of the professed aims of specialist firms like Triodos bank, as well as the ethical products of the more mainstream local companies such as AXA Sun Life and Clerical Medical, is to have a positive impact on such issues as wealth disparity, deprivation, social polarisation and the perceived degradation of civic culture. Indeed, the very insistence that social and environmental

---

[14] In addition to the work in Barton Hill, other groups have also sought to highlight the problem of financial exclusion in Bristol. For instance ACT, a Bristol-based community group, has through the auspices of the national Citizen Organising Foundation (COF) sought to lobby the high-street banks, the British Bankers Association and the Bank of England about the problem of financial exclusion in deprived areas of south Bristol such as Hartcliffe (www.activetogether.org/background/cof.html).

sustainability and other similar criteria need to be taken into account when making lending and investment decisions can itself be interpreted as an attempt to reassert the need for a moral order, a common set of values to fill the existing moral void. However, it is very difficult to assess the specific impact of such providers on social cohesion in Bristol. Although money has been directly lent to local businesses and projects by Triodos, for instance, the bank provides business finance to companies right throughout the UK. Similarly, the impact on social cohesion in a particular place such as Bristol of specific investment positions (such as the SRI investment funds Holden Meehan advises on, or the equity held by the ethical stockbrokers Rathbone Neilson) is both extremely difficult to trace and to assess. What is clear is that just as the SRI sector is still small in comparison to mainstream investment and lending activities, so its proportionate effect in comparison to wider competitive processes contributing to financial exclusion is likely to be relative. Having said this, and as noted earlier in this chapter, the number and value of SRI funds have significantly increased over the last few years and thus the influence of SRI, itself shaped and influenced by actors and institutions in Bristol, on social cohesion has accordingly grown.

Conclusion: shaping the future of finance

As we highlighted at the very beginning of this chapter, the local growth of Bristol's financial services sector during the 1970s and 1980s owes a great deal to processes of decentralisation from London. In particular, Bristol benefited greatly from the decision of a number of retail financial services providers, particularly insurance companies, to relocate activities to the city and surrounds. The subsequent concentration of financial service activity has itself attracted and fostered new start-up operations, particularly in insurance. By the early 1990s, however, the city could no longer rely on large-scale relocations to continue to fuel growth. In addition, the increasingly competitive nature of the financial service's market-place, together with new opportunities for restructuring and rationalising both 'front-office' and 'back-office' operations also placed

pressure on the future of those activities already located in Bristol.

The primary aim of this chapter has been to examine how well Bristol has competed in the face of the challenges of the last decade. Despite the relative decline in its status since 1991, from fifth to sixth largest financial centre in the UK, analysis of employment data shows that the total number of people employed in financial services in Bristol has remained quite constant. Our study suggests that in the face of processes of market consolidation and of IT-driven rationalisation, restructuring and the development of new delivery channels, Bristol has up until now still managed to retain jobs and activities. Explanations of why this has been the case highlight a number of competitive assets:

1. sunk costs, in terms of labour and office space;
2. urban and city assets, in terms of communication linkages, an attractive environment and access to regional markets;
3. evidence of traded interdependencies (Storper, 1995) in the servicing of this regional market, particularly with regard to corporate or commercial financial services;
4. evidence of untraded interdependencies (Storper, 1995) helping to constitute a local pool of labour expertise in the insurance, especially life insurance, and to a lesser extent retail banking and mortgage sectors.

In addition, drawing on a strong local social and environmental institutional thickness, Bristol has developed particular expertise in the growing SRI sector.

Despite Bristol's relative success in locking in place existing activity and adapting to new innovative markets and methods of delivery, the city failed to take advantage of the resurgence in employment in financial services in the late 1990s to the same extent as other regional financial centres. Among other factors, our study found that Bristol has been constrained by the availability of suitable labour. The problem of a supply of skilled labour is one in which local government could clearly play an important role. However, strategies designed to address this issue must also critically take into account the growing number of financial services providers seeking to relocate call centre and other back-office jobs, not to lower-cost locations in the UK, but to lower-cost locations overseas, in particular India. There is an obvious danger that policy initiatives designed to address the gap between local demand and supply of back-office and call centre jobs will rapidly become irrelevant in the face of the relocation of such activity. Having said that, our study has highlighted some grounds for optimism in Bristol's capacity to hold onto a proportion of these jobs. The range of factors outlined above, including the desire to minimise risk, has helped Bristol retain existing jobs and create jobs in new telephone-based service delivery in the face of lower-cost competition in the UK. Similarly, we argue that it is likely, particularly in the case of the many smaller call centre operations, that these same factors will at the very least mitigate against the wholesale relocation of such activities overseas, certainly in the short to medium term. In addition to policies, including training schemes, aimed at supporting existing call centres, local government could play an important role in supporting and encouraging existing and new high value-added activity. So, for instance, supporting the development of the SRI sector and encouraging linkages and the development of business synergies between local SRI providers and local life companies. Further, there is a potential role for local government in supporting existing local networking and institutionalism (French, 2000, 2002) in the life assurance 'cluster' (DTI, 2001) and encouraging the development of institutional thickness (Amin and Thrift, 1995) in other sectors. In the face of continued processes of 'regionalisation', there must also be renewed effort, both in terms of the provision of urban infrastructure and in terms of business and public perception, to secure Bristol's position as the regional capital of the South West.

5

City of culture?

Keith Bassett, Ron Griffiths and Ian Smith

The concept of culture is notoriously elusive, partly since cultural processes are so pervasive, and partly because culture and related terms carry such a wide range of meanings, rooted in different intellectual traditions. In its broadest sense, the cultural domain encompasses those social processes that are primarily concerned with the creation and communication of meaning and the formation of identity – be that through the traditional 'high' arts, popular music, community festivals, architecture, advertising, fashion, or any of the diverse ways in which meanings are socially circulated. However defined, commentators are generally agreed that cultural processes have in recent decades come to assume a much greater prominence in a range of different spheres. Culture, it is argued, has become more central as a focus of personal life, a source of economic prosperity, a field of social contestation, and as an object of policy at all levels of governance (Featherstone, 1991; Keith and Pile, 1993; Lash and Urry, 1994; McGuigan, 1996). Nowhere has this been more apparent than at the level of the city. As cities in the developed world have struggled to cope with de-industrialisation, the globalisation of economic power and deepening social divides, attention has increasingly turned to the role that culture can play in fostering economic competitiveness and social cohesion (Zukin, 1995; Scott, 2000). Cultural processes of various kinds have thus come to be seen as central to the economic and social health of cities, and urban cultural policies have accordingly grown in their scope and importance.

The harnessing of culture for purposes of urban regeneration has taken a number of different forms, each reflecting different aspects of the cultural domain. For example, since the 1980s a wave of new, high-profile arts and entertainment *venues* have been developed as cities have sought to refashion their images, clean up marginal spaces, and promote themselves in the competition for mobile investment and tourism revenues. Investment has been channelled into cultural and sporting *events*, with a view both to attracting external audiences and fostering civic identity and cohesion among local populations. Cities have put their social history, architecture and physical landscapes under the microscope in the search for *heritage resources* that can be used to gain symbolic advantage over their competitors. Commercial *cultural products industries*, in such fields as fashion, music recording and broadcasting, have been identified as drivers of post-industrial economic development, and have consequently become the somewhat bemused target of interventions by public policy makers. *Participation in artistic activity* has been recognised as a potentially powerful tool for building the self-confidence and social integration of isolated and excluded groups and communities.

Cities attempting to employ culture for economic, social and physical ends have typically made use of a blend of different approaches. In Birmingham, for example, a number of new high-profile arts and entertainment venues and public art works have acted as important catalysts for the extensive remodelling and upgrading of the city centre since the 1990s. However, the city has also capitalised on its industrial heritage, most notably by 'theming' its jewellery quarter as a venue for tourism and speciality shopping. There have also been initiatives to convert old industrial buildings into workspaces for micro-firms operating in the commercial cultural industries. As another example, Glasgow is perhaps the leading exemplar of a city that has used a programme of cultural events, staged during its tenure in 1990 as European City of Culture, as a strategy to turn around its negative image and position itself as a leading destination for urban cultural tourism. It has also invested substantially in the building of new arts venues and promoted its role as a centre of the design industries. Other cities, such as Sheffield, Manchester, Newcastle and Liverpool, have similarly given prominence to broad-based cultural strategies as tools of urban regeneration.

It was against this background that the research programme for the Bristol Integrated City Study (ICS) was drawn up in 1997. The arts and media sectors have commonly been cited as one of Bristol's distinctive assets. Particular strengths have been attributed to the city in certain fields, notably television programme making and popular music. In the early 1990s, a new emphasis was given to culture by the city's civic leaders. A cultural strategy for the city was drawn up, and a new lead agency (the Bristol Cultural Development Partnership) was established to take the strategy forward. Given this context, it was judged that the arts and cultural industries should be one of the main strands within the Bristol ICS research programme, in the belief that the Bristol study would provide an effective setting for building a deeper understanding of the role that the cultural sector can play in fostering competitiveness and cohesion in cities.

This chapter summarises some of the findings of this aspect of the study. It begins with an overview of the city's cultural sector and the development of cultural policies. It then considers in more detail three contrasting aspects of recent cultural development in the city, relating to the film and television industries; investments in new arts and entertainment infrastructure in the city centre; and the role of the arts in neighbourhood renewal. The chapter concludes with an assessment of the role that cultural development has played in the city since the early 1990s.

Bristol's cultural sector

In order to consider the role of Bristol's 'cultural sector' within the city-region, one needs to consider both the city's role in the consumption of culture (as a location for theatres, galleries, concert venues, and

so on) and its role in the production of culture (as a location for television and film production, for example). Each of these aspects of being a cultural city is reflected in the physical infrastructure, cultural outputs and employment patterns in the city.

It is difficult to identify a set of precise cultural indicators that would allow a detailed comparison between Bristol and other large English cities, due to the lack or unreliability of data (see Selwood, 2001). Here we will mainly focus on employment totals and elements of physical infrastructure as measures of Bristol's cultural standing.

Table 5.1 summarises the employment associated with different components of the cultural sector. The bundle of activities labelled as cultural production and media includes employment in television, radio and film production; advertising and miscellaneous computer-related activities (including new media); and numbers of artists and artistes. The Bristol total is 8,300 jobs, of which 2,900 are in film, radio and television production. The concentration of employment in these activities was nearly three times the national average (with location quotients of 1.4 and 2.17 respectively). Comparing Bristol with cities divided up in relation to location in the urban hierarchy of Britain, it is clear that the relative concentration of employment in these activities is only surpassed by Greater London, with Bristol accounting for about one fifth of all employment in film, radio and television production in the large dominant cities across Britain. However, within activities related to cultural consumption (employment in bookshops, theatres, cinemas, other performance venues, museums and libraries), there is a clear under-representation of employment both in comparison to the national average as well as relative to other large dominant cities.

The economic vibrancy of the cultural sector can be caught through a comparison of the growth rates for various economic sectors (Table 5.2). Growth rates are shown for activities related to cultural production and consumption (as defined earlier in this chapter) and are compared to growth rates for all sectors combined (excluding agriculture and fisheries) and the growth in the broader category of financial, property and business services. Table 5.2 shows that over the five-year period of 1995-2001 there was an estimated growth in Bristol of about 2,800 jobs in

Table 5.1: Employment impact of cultural industries in Bristol and the rest of Britain (2001)

	Total employment 2001[7]			Location quotient 2001[7]		
	Cultural production and media[4]	Cultural consumption (visitor-related)[5]	Film, radio and television production[6]	Cultural production and media[4]	Cultural consumption (visitor-related)[5]	Film, radio and television production[6]
Bristol	8,300	14,900	2,900	1.40	0.83	2.17
Greater London[1]	173,700	222,600	49,900	2.46	1.04	3.17
Major northern cities[2]	32,800	111,200	7,800	0.84	0.94	0.89
Large dominant cities[3,8]	58,800	246,600	11,500	0.72	0.99	0.63
Sub-dominant cities[3]	54,300	191,100	6,000	0.80	0.93	0.40
Medium-sized towns[3]	17,000	112,200	1,600	0.47	1.03	0.20
Sub-dominant towns[3]	32,000	139,800	7,900	0.67	0.96	0.73

Notes:
[1] London and Heathrow travel-to-work areas (1984 revision).
[2] Liverpool, Manchester, Birmingham and Glasgow (1984 revision).
[3] Classification of travel-to-work areas outlined in Green and Owen (1990; 1984 revision).
[4] Includes SIC classes 7260, 7440, 7481, 9211, 9212, 9220 and 9231.
[5] Includes SIC classes 5247, 5530, 5540, 9213, 9232, 9251 and 9252.
[6] Includes SIC classes 9211 and 9220.
[7] Based on averaging figures from ABI 2000 and 2001.
[8] Excludes the figures for Bristol (classified as a large dominant city).
Source: Annual Business Inquiry (ABI) (2000, 2001) National Statistics

cultural production as a whole (49%), although only 200 of these are accounted for in film, radio and television production (a 7% increase). This compares to a growth rate of 11% for all financial, property and business services. This pattern of growth for Bristol, however, is exceeded by all other parts of the urban hierarchy, although the data suggests that employment change within activities related to cultural consumption (cultural venues, bars and restaurants) is higher in Bristol than for other parts of the urban hierarchy.

Turning now to measures of physical infrastructure, we can generate a different set of comparisons. The Core Cities Group report of August 1999 (CCG, 1999) indicated that within the seven core cities of England (of which Bristol is one) there is an under-provision of theatres, concert halls and cinemas relative to their population size and relative to England as a whole. Instead of being the location for an expected 25% of the national total of these venues, the core cities only provided about 20% of the national total (although they were the location for 40% of these venues within their city-regions). In Bristol itself, the most notable lack has been a large, modern concert hall to complement or replace the ageing Colston Hall. In terms of cinema capacity, Bristol has 35.5 cinema seats per 1,000 head of population, in comparison to an average of 20.9 seats per 1,000 head for all English large dominant cities.

In terms of local museums, Bristol records an above-average number of visits per head of population and operates these museums at a cost-efficient level (based on comparing best value indicators for Bristol and 13 other large dominant cities).

Table 5.3 provides more details of the relative provision of various types of arts venues for the Bristol city centre, suburban areas, and the rest of the city-region (including Bath and Weston-super-Mare). In terms of theatres, concert halls and cinemas, the core city of Bristol (incorporating both the city centre and the suburbs) accounts for 60-70% of venues for the city-region as a whole. However, the city-centre itself only provides around one third of these venues, with multiplex cinemas much more strongly represented in suburban Bristol. Also, although the core city is a strong focus as the location of public arts venues, there is a strong tendency for private arts dealers to cluster elsewhere in the city-region, mainly within the central area of Bath (which accounts for over 50% of private galleries). A concentration of artistic and tourist-related activities in Bath is of little surprise given the World Heritage status of the city.

In addition to being the location of arts and cultural venues, Bristol city is also an important location for a series of festivals linked to different categories of film production (natural history, animated, and 'short' films

Table 5.2: Employment change in cultural industries in Bristol and the rest of Britain (1995-2001)

	% employment change 1995-2001[9]				
	Cultural production and media[4]	Cultural consumption (visitor-related)[5]	Film, radio and television production[6]	Financial, property and business services[7]	All non-agricultural employment[8]
Bristol	49.2	17.9	7.5	10.9	12.8
Greater London[1]	50.6	13.7	23.3	32.8	16.6
Major northern cities[2]	34.3	9.0	22.6	24.6	10.5
Large dominant cities[3,10]	53.6	7.1	27.7	25.1	8.1
Sub-dominant cities[3]	66.1	9.5	46.4	30.1	11.9
Medium-sized towns[3]	67.5	9.6	10.0	23.4	9.6
Sub-dominant towns[3]	113.5	10.5	348.0	23.2	9.6

Notes:
[1] London and Heathrow travel-to-work areas (1984 revision).
[2] Liverpool, Manchester, Birmingham and Glasgow (1984 revision).
[3] Classification of travel-to-work areas outlined in Green and Owen (1990; 1984 revision).
[4] Includes SIC classes 7260, 7440, 7481, 9211, 9212, 9220 and 9231.
[5] Includes SIC classes 5247, 5530, 5540, 9213, 9232, 9251 and 9252.
[6] Includes SIC classes 9211 and 9220.
[7] Includes SIC divisions 65-74.
[8] Includes SIC division 10-99.
[9] Based on averaging AES (rescaled) figures for 1995 and 1996, ABI figures for 2000 and 2001.
[10] Excludes figures for Bristol (a large dominant city).
Source: Annual Business Inquiry (ABI) (2000, 2001); Annual Employment Survey (AES) (rescaled) (1995, 1996) National Statistics

in general), ballooning, popular music, and maritime events centred on the historic harbour. The St Paul's Street Carnival is also one of the largest outside London.

Overall, then, Bristol plays a dominant cultural role in the city-region, although it shares important functions with Bath, which has its own strengths in publishing and private arts dealing. Although the totals for employment in the cultural sector are not high compared with some other employment sectors in the city, rates of growth have been high, and Bristol does have an important cluster of activities related to television and film production that is of much more than regional importance.

The emergence of a strategy for culture

During the 1980s, civic leaders in many British cities began to recognise the strategic importance of their cultural sectors, and to make substantial political and financial investments aimed at strengthening their cultural infrastructure. However, the attitude towards the cultural sector of Bristol's civic leadership at that time was more apathetic. Indeed, an arts development officer commented in an interview that, when she came to the city in the mid-1980s, "Bristol city council was inactive in the arts".

Table 5.3: Location of arts venues within the Bristol city-region

		Bristol city centre	Suburban Bristol	Rest of city-region
All cinemas	Number of cinemas	5	6	6
	Number of screens	8	59	12
Independent/arts cinemas	Number of cinemas	3	0	4
	Number of screens	4	0	7
Theatres, concert halls and public art galleries (number)		8	6	7
Private art galleries and dealers (number of businesses)		4	14	27

One of the consequences of the lack of civic leadership in the cultural sphere was that, by the beginning of the 1990s, Bristol's cultural organisations had experienced a series of major funding crises. There was also a number of widely acknowledged weaknesses in terms of the city's cultural and sporting infrastructure. There are several factors that help to account for the city's relative backwardness in cultural policy at that time. They include the division of local government responsibilities in the sub-region and the political rivalries between Bristol and Avon; the comparative dynamism of the city's main economic sectors, which put less pressure on local decision makers to seek alternative sources of growth; and the lack of access to regional funds.

A major shift in policy came in the early 1990s, propelled by several pressures. First, the Bristol economy experienced a sudden (if temporary) downturn, with the result that civic leaders suddenly became more receptive to arguments about the strategic importance of the cultural sector, especially in the context of their heightened interest in positioning Bristol as a leading European city. Second, the regional arts body, South West Arts (SWA), had been reinvigorated by the devolution of arts funding and made it a priority to encourage the city council to give more serious attention to its role in culture and the arts. Third, significant moves were also taking place in some sections of the business community to forge better working relations with the city council, in the wake of a long period of often bitter conflict and mistrust. A new 'business leadership team', The Bristol Initiative (TBI), joined forces with SWA to encourage the city council to collaborate with them in commissioning a major review of the cultural sector in the city by a team of consultants. The review, *A cultural strategy for Bristol*, was published in 1992 (Boyden Southwood Associates, 1992). As well as providing a detailed cultural audit, the report argued that cultural strategy needed to be "much more than just an arts plan" (Boyden Southwood Associates, 1992, p 4). Culture, it argued, had a strategic role to play in making a city "distinctive" and attractive to visitors and investors. It was a "key organising principle informing how cities plan for their future" (1992, p 4).

One of the report's core proposals, for a cultural strategy unit, led to the setting up of the Bristol Cultural Development Partnership (BCDP), consisting mainly of representatives of local business, the city council, and SWA. A head of cultural development was recruited from outside the city in 1993, and the partnership, although operating with restricted funds, played an energetic and increasingly important catalytic role in attracting festivals and cultural investment in the city. This new momentum in cultural policy continued through the early to mid-1990s. On the media front, the opening of offices in the city for a new South West Media Development Agency (SWMDA), together with a branch office of the South West Film Commission (SWFC), was an important further addition to the city's institutional apparatus for cultural policy.

Although the period 1991-97 contained signs of a real cultural revival in the city, there were also a number of important setbacks and disappointments for cultural policy makers. For example, a joint bid with Bath to host the Year of Photography and the Electronic Image under the Arts Council's Arts 2000 scheme was unsuccessful. Another major project, to secure resources from the Arts Council's stabilisation fund to underpin development plans for the city's three main cultural flagships (Bristol Old Vic, Arnolfini and Watershed) also met with failure. A major reorganisation of local government in the sub-region in 1996 also resulted in disappointment. The upper-tier body, Avon County Council, was removed, to be replaced not by a unitary Greater Bristol Authority, but by four separate unitaries, with the city council boundary retained in its existing form. This did nothing to solve the problem that the city was endeavouring to play a sub-regional role in cultural terms, but without the resources to fund it.

Then in 1997, the development of new cultural infrastructures in the area of the city docks, funded by National Lottery money through the Millennium Commission and the Arts Council, was hit by the sudden decision by the Arts Council not to support a planned centre for the performing arts, for which design work was now well-advanced (see later in this chapter for a more detailed discussion). In the words of one leading figure in the local cultural policy network, the loss of the performing arts centre, the 'jewel in the crown' of what was to be a new cultural quarter, was "a serious blow not just to the arts in the city", but also to enthusiasm for partnership working more generally.

There was also a shift underway in the centre of gravity of cultural policy in the city towards a stronger local authority role. From being an organisation that according to a member of one of the city's main cultural bodies, had "never thought of things corporately", and shown a "lack of commitment and general miserliness towards the arts", the city council was now seeing the cultural sector as an integral part of an emerging corporate vision and a new approach to strategic planning. This shift was partly in response to changes in the national policy context, such as a change in emphasis in government thinking on urban regeneration, with the former reliance on property-led approaches and 'trickle-down' benefits being replaced by a new rhetoric of community-led partnerships to counter social exclusion. Another factor was the new emphasis of the Department for Culture, Media and Sport (DCMS) on adopting a broad, inclusive, conception of culture, and aligning policy in the culture field with the government's wider economic regeneration, social cohesion and lifelong learning objectives.

Personnel changes within the council were also significant. A new director of leisure services had been appointed in 1997, and brought with him a fresh determination to realise Bristol's potential as a cultural centre. These ambitions were assisted by the fact that, over the period 1998-2000, the city council embarked on a major programme of internal reorganisation, partly designed to strengthen the council's capacity for strategic policy making and combat narrow departmentalism and inter-service rivalry. At the member level, a cabinet model of political leadership was put into place, and at officer level, existing directorates were brought together to form five super-departments. In a deliberate attempt to cement the linkage between culture and regeneration, the cluster of services in the former leisure services directorate (arts, sport, libraries, museums, parks and heritage) were kept together, and combined with two other key regeneration-oriented directorates: planning and transport. It was an organisational arrangement that dovetailed closely with the aspirations of the council's recently appointed director of leisure services, who was chosen as the head of the new Department of Environment, Transport and Leisure.

Another key part of this new phase was the strengthening of the regional agenda. With the prospect of the new Regional Development Agency (RDA) for the South West region, the main cultural agencies came together to form a Cultural Agencies Group (CAG), which provided the foundation for the DCMS-sponsored Regional Cultural Consortium, formed in 1999. There were also moves to create a stronger regional dimension to the National Lottery, and to strengthen further the role of the regional arts board.

This phase of policy was also marked by a further break from the council's record of 'miserliness' and 'complacency' in cultural policy, as accumulated debts of almost £1 million were written off to enable the Watershed to secure stabilisation funding from the Arts Council, and an enhanced package of funding support was agreed with the Bristol Old Vic. Another aspect was a new concern to understand, and foster, the wider cultural 'ecology' of the city, including the linkages between the flagship institutions, local arts and community-based cultural activity. In a further sign of the impact of the DCMS agenda, the city council also took some initial steps towards asserting a strategic role for itself in the development of the media sector (Bristol City Council, 2000).

It can be seen, therefore, that Bristol made significant progress in cultural policy terms in the decade from 1992 to 2002. In the first phase, leadership rested with a number of specially constituted partnership bodies. These largely followed an agenda of 'city boosterism', which met with a mixture of outstanding success and dashed hopes. More recently, a stronger lead has been taken by the city council, influenced by important changes in the national policy landscape, involving a broader conception of the cultural field and more encouragement to link arts and culture to other policy areas. Against the background of this survey of the city's evolving strategy for culture, this chapter now turns to a more detailed examination of three contrasting aspects of cultural development in the city over the last decade: the commercial cultural industries; cultural infrastructures and city-centre regeneration; and the role of the arts in community development and social inclusion.

Cultural industries in Bristol

The cultural (or creative) products industries have attracted increasing attention from researchers and policy makers in recent years, not least because of their evident importance to employment and economic growth (for example, Creative Industries Task Force, 1998; Scott, 2000). Although the products of cultural industries are often distributed by large, multinational media corporations, production is often carried out by small, interdependent firms in localised, spatial clusters. While the major clusters are found in large world cities such as London, Paris and Los Angeles, there is some evidence that certain favoured cities further down the urban hierarchy may be able to sustain smaller, more specialised, clusters of activity. Bristol, which increasingly attempts to market itself as Britain's 'second media city', is a case in point (Griffiths et al, 1999; Bristol City Council, 2000).

A DTI report on industrial clusters in the UK (DTI, 2001) revealed the overwhelming dominance of London with respect to the location of cultural industries in the UK, but also identified an 'embryonic' television and digital media cluster of international significance in the South West, but largely concentrated in Bristol. This cultural cluster includes the two big employers, BBC Bristol and HTV West, which are major regional production centres for television and radio, and also a range of smaller media companies. However, when we examine this broad cluster in more detail, it separates into several mini-clusters, the most notable centring around natural history film making and 3D animation.

Natural history film making

Bristol claims to be a world centre for the making of wildlife and natural history films and has cultivated its image as "the green Hollywood", "the home to more wildlife TV specialists than any other city on Earth" (publicity material for 2000 Wildscreen film festival in Bristol). Assessing this claim involves looking at the structure of natural history film production, its trajectory over time, and the internal relations and dynamics of the cluster.

The cluster centres on the BBC's Natural History Unit (NHU), the historic core of the cluster since its establishment, almost by historical accident, in 1957 (Parsons, 1982; Davies, 2000a). The unit expanded along with the expansion of television channels and audiences and has been responsible for major wildlife series, including *The world about us*, which ran for almost 20 years, and *Life on Earth*, narrated by David Attenborough, which reached a worldwide audience in the 1980s.

In the 1990s, significant changes resulted from a mixture of broadcasting deregulation, new managerial regimes at the BBC, new filming and broadcasting technologies, and changes in audience demand. The 1990 Broadcasting Act, for example, which required the BBC and the independent television companies to buy in at least 25% of their total programme output from independent companies, encouraged the setting up of new, small companies, particularly by ex-BBC staff, to provide specialist programmes and facilities. Nevertheless, the NHU maintained its dominant position, particularly in the production of expensive, 'blue-chip' series with high production values and a long shelf life that could be sold worldwide. By 2000, the NHU could claim to be the largest wildlife film production unit in the world, employing around 300 people within the larger BBC complex in the city (Davies, 2000b).

The HTV studios also became the home of Partridge Films, the next largest film production unit in the city. Originally founded in London, the company became part of United Wildlife, and more recently has become the core of Granada's wildlife unit, Granada Wild. Smaller but internationally famous production companies, such as Green Umbrella, Tigress, Scorer, Zebra, and Beeley Productions, which were variously established often by ex-BBC employees in the 1980s and early 1990s, are found in close proximity to the BBC in the Clifton area of the city. Although they provide programmes for the BBC and HTV channels, much of their more recent output has been for the US market.

Wildlife film making is a complex process, and although most of the filming is carried out abroad, much of the post-production work is carried out in Bristol, either within the BBC and HTV studios, or by smaller independent companies and freelancers. Thus, both the NHU and the independent production companies use the facilities provided by a range of specialist post-production companies such as

4.2.2. Videographics, Films at 59, and Bristol Film and Video (BFV). These facilities grew rapidly in the 1990s, and in most cases were also started by ex-BBC employees. Finally, around these companies has extended a wider, shifting network of individual freelancers, subcontracted for specialist tasks such as camerawork, soundtracking, editing and music composing. Some of the small production companies, for example, might expand and contract from a handful of key personnel to as many as 40 or 50 workers as projects are started or finished.

The various production and post-production companies within the cluster are tied together by *traded interdependencies* (such as commissioning and subcontracting relationships) and *untraded interdependencies* (involving social contacts and networks which provide vital sources of information in a fast changing market). Although the Bristol media community is small compared to the community in London, similar importance is attached to informal social contacts (in local eateries and bars on Whiteladies Road, Clifton, for example) and spatial proximity. As one independent producer put it:

> "The costs of being in Clifton are relatively high compared to being elsewhere in Bristol, but you couldn't possibly be anywhere else because that is where the BBC is ... ecause that is where all the production and post-production houses are."

In the words of another:

> "When we looked for this office, I just put a pin in the BBC and drew 50 yards around it."

The cluster is strengthened and further embedded in the city by the presence of specialised *institutional supports*, such as the bi-annual Wildscreen Festival, one of the leading international, wildlife film festivals, which attracts around 900 delegates to the city. The festival's ties to the city have been strengthened by the recent completion of the Wildwalk complex, with an IMAX cinema, in the central Harbourside area (discussed later in this chapter).

Also important in consolidating the local cluster has been the construction of formal, technical networks between local firms such as the Bristol Creative Technology Network, an optical fibre network which uses the latest broadband technology to link together local firms and university computer and design departments.

Although this cluster of activities grew rapidly in the 1980s and early 1990s, the growth trajectory levelled off in the late 1990s, and recent patterns of change appear to reflect a complex of cyclical and structural factors. Both the NHU and Partridge Films have survived corporate restructuring within the BBC and the takeover of HTV by Granada, although both now find themselves facing increased competitive pressures. The smaller production companies have been particularly affected by a downturn in the level of demand for natural history programmes, which has forced most of them to drastically cut their workforces. One of the post-production facilities, BFV, has gone (perhaps temporarily) out of business. There has also been evidence of changes in the structure of demand for natural history programmes, with traditional blue-chip programmes and series increasingly displaced by more 'story-driven' animal dramas and 'celebrities-meet-animals' programmes. Such changes, along with the proliferation of channels and the fragmentation of audiences, poses particular threats to blue-chip producers, such as the NHU. All firms within the sector are also faced with uncertainties over the impacts of new broadcasting technologies, such as high-definition television, interactive television, and the convergence between television and the Internet which would enable programmes of choice to be downloaded at will in any order.

Animation

The growth of an animation cluster has been much more recent, and although still small in terms of employment and the number of firms, it has great symbolic and publicity value for the city.

The general picture of the animation industry in the UK is of a sector with a few large-scale studios and a much larger mass of small production companies and freelancers, heavily concentrated in London. However, recent growth in Bristol has enabled the city to stake a claim to be the second largest centre in the UK and one of the most important centres in Europe, with local firms estimated to have an annual turnover of £60 million in 2000. The city is certainly the leading centre for 3D stop-frame animation and the home of some of the most famous and creative animators working today. Most of the firms are small, and located near the old docks, or in the Old Market area of the city, a different pattern of concentration to the natural history production companies which are clustered around the BBC in Clifton.

The largest company is Aardman Animations, now one of Bristol's highest-profile companies, and the main reason why Bristol is a centre for animation. The company was originally formed in 1972, and became particularly well known for its Wallace and Gromit films. However, its largest income came from television advertising work until it secured a £150m deal with Spielberg's Dreamworks company to produce three feature-length films, the first of which was the highly successful *Chicken run*. The company expanded in 2000 to three sites, in the central area and the northern periphery.

The other production companies that have grown up around Aardman are much smaller, although no less innovative. They include A for Animation, bolexbrothers, Fictitious Egg, Elm Road Studios, the BBC Animation Unit, and 4.2.2.Videographics. In addition to these production companies, there are various specialist firms, such as Cod Steaks and Farington Lewis, that have grown up to provide necessary inputs to the production process, such as scenery, backdrops and models. The local cluster also includes "a very big, very talented freelance base of model makers, animators and set builders that different companies draw upon" (comment from animator in the BBC Animation Unit, *Western Daily Press*, 19 May 2000).

An important support for the cluster is provided by highly rated training courses for animators offered by Bristol Mediaworks (part of the University of the West of England), and the presence in the city of an internationally important animation festival, Animated Encounters, which returned to Bristol in 2000, after being lost to Cardiff in the 1980s.

However, as with most media sectors, this is a highly volatile industry, subject to rapid changes in demand and technological innovation. In 2001, for example, Aardman was forced to axe 150 jobs after scrapping its first script for its contracted feature-length film to follow *Chicken run*.

In contrast to the wildlife sub-sector, animation is markedly less dependent on Bristol-based post-production facilities, with firms looking more to London for specialist services. This is partly a result of the particular mechanics of animation production, and partly because of the preferences of advertising companies, who are major clients of animation companies.

In summary, although small in many respects, these Bristol media clusters have international significance in their specialist fields, and their presence shows that smaller cities like Bristol, further down the urban hierarchy than world cities, can still be important sites of self-sustaining cultural production (when based on high-quality outputs in specialist sectors, and when conditions have enabled such networks of interdependencies to become embedded in a locality). However, our analysis also points to the threats posed by the volatility of markets, the local fallouts from corporate restructuring, and the pace of technological change. Bristol's role in these sub-sectors cannot be taken for granted.

Cultural infrastructures and inner-city regeneration

City governments in the US and Europe have for some time been attracted to the idea of using investment in cultural infrastructures – such as prestige concert halls, museums and art galleries – as catalysts for urban regeneration, particularly in inner-city areas. Such a mobilisation of culture in the service of urban growth and regeneration has also proved popular with coalitions of urban elites and served as foci for partnership activities. Projects of this kind can be highly successful; however, in some cases they have proved controversial, particularly when such prestige projects have relied on the heavy use of public funds and created little more than 'scenic enclaves' for middle-class consumption.

Bristol's Harbourside, enthusiastically described by English Partnerships as "one of Europe's most exciting urban renewal schemes" (Bristol 2000, undated), is an example of such culture-led regeneration, and has likewise proved both highly successful and controversial at the same time. The area in question is part of Bristol's historic harbour, which lies in the heart of the city. The harbour was important in mediaeval times, but commercial shipping had virtually ceased by the 1960s. The city was thus left with a large area of increasingly derelict dockland close to the heart of the city. From the 1970s onwards, much of this dockland area was redeveloped through a series of schemes for housing and leisure activities, but the conversion of dockside warehouses into cultural spaces, such as the Arnolfini arts complex and the Watershed Media Centre, also had important catalytic affects. However, in spite of a succession of plans and projects, one of the key sites in the docks, Canons Marsh, still lay largely derelict in the early 1990s.

The Harbourside scheme, as it came to be called, emerged out of the changed political and economic context of the early 1990s, when the downturn in the local economy and charges of municipal complacency led to a series of business-led initiatives and the launching of a widening array of public–private partnerships (Bassett, 1996; Stewart, 1996). As noted earlier, one of the earliest manifestations of this new spirit of partnership was the commissioning of a major study of the cultural sector in Bristol. One of the key recommendations in the study's final report was that 'flagship' cultural projects should be used to create a new cultural district in the Canons Marsh area (Boyden Southwood Associates, 1992). The inclusion of major cultural elements was seen as having a number of potential benefits: acting as a catalyst for private investment, strengthening the role of the city centre in competing with out-of-town developments, and underlining the city's bid for international status.

The enlarged Bristol Chamber of Commerce and Initiative (BCCI) played a key role in promoting this plan, and in 1993 helped to bring together the private landowners and the city council as the Harbourside Sponsors Group with an agreed framework for the development for Canons Marsh. English Partnerships, the government's urban regeneration agency, committed funds for feasibility work, and the council issued a revised and more developer-friendly planning brief for the site. However, large-scale, culture-led regeneration depended on much more funding than the council could provide or developers were prepared to spend at that time.

The potential for closing this funding gap came in 1995 when the National Lottery was launched, opening up significant new possibilities for culture-led regeneration through its arts and millennium funds. The BCDP took a leading role in quickly putting together linked bids for three major cultural projects. The first was for a 'hands-on' science museum based on the existing 'Exploratory', originally founded in 1983 by the scientist Richard Gregory, which had been surviving in a succession of temporary quarters in the city. The second was a project for an 'electronic zoo' and wildlife film archive which was the brainchild of a former head of the BBC NHU. A new partnership, Bristol 2000, was formed, headed by the chairman of Wessex Water, to bid for Millennium Lottery Funding for these projects. In parallel, another partnership was formed, headed by the chairman of HTV, to put forward an even more ambitious project to replace the city's ageing Colston Hall with a dramatic new centre for the performing arts on the waterfront, designed by leading German architects.

In 1996 the city was successful in being awarded £41 million of grants from the Millennium Commission towards the cost of building the science and wildlife projects (now called Explore and Wildwalk), with the various parties involved bound together through a complex financial arrangement in which part of the profits from the commercial part of the site would go towards the essential matching funding for the cultural infrastructures and public spaces. As a result, in its 1998 review of progress in the city, the BCCI singled out the waterfront as the site for "the most striking result of partnership working" (Adburgham, 1998, p 15), symbolising "how confrontation within the city has transmuted into co-operation" (p 60).

However, the city suffered a blow in 1998 when funding for the Centre for the Performing Arts (CPA) was suddenly withdrawn following the change in government, a change in National Lottery rules, and a tougher attitude towards capital projects implemented by the new chairman of the Arts Council. The Arts Council justified its cancellation on the basis of what it saw as inadequate business planning, audience research, public consultation and leadership. However, local business and political leaders responded by accusing the Arts Council of "betrayal" and sending in a "hit squad" to rubbish the project in order to save money. Although the city's

Members of Parliaments lobbied other government ministers, the coalition behind the project quickly conceded defeat among some mutual recrimination.

However, the two millennium projects were opened in April 2000 and substantially exceeded their visitor expectations in the first year of operation. Bristol has also acquired a major new square, Millennium Square, and a striking new footbridge linking the cultural projects to the city centre. These have been notable achievements after nearly 30 years of failed plans and projects on the site.

However, the catalytic role of the cultural projects in bringing forward the development of the rest of the site has proved more uncertain. The contract for development was awarded to Crest Nicholson, a development company, which brought forward a plan for a mixture of housing, retailing, offices, public spaces, and a leisure and cinema complex. The scheme proved highly controversial, partly on design grounds including the blocking of views to the cathedral, but also because of its content. The make-up of the cultural elements has been one of the sources of the controversy, with claims from some quarters that a proposed multiplex cinema would attract 'unwelcome elements' into the area. A second scheme was drawn up in response to criticisms, but it aroused even more opposition from the city's highly vocal and well-organised amenity and conservation groups, backed by the local press. After failing to get outline planning permission, Crest had to drop its original architects, appoint a new master planner, and engage a consultancy to carry out a highly elaborate consultation procedure with local 'stakeholders' and the general public. Finally, in late 2001, the company obtained planning permission at its third attempt (see Bassett et al, 2002, for a detailed account and analysis).

Overall, then, the new cultural projects have been largely successful in themselves, although the failure to get a new centre for the performing arts remains a major disappointment, and the expected catalytic effect on the surrounding areas has proved much more conflict prone than expected.

The arts, community development and social inclusion

We have seen that cultural strategy in Bristol in the 1990s was mainly concerned with using culture for economic and physical regeneration purposes, tied to the city's ambitions to achieve European city status. In the latter half of the decade, however, there were signs of a growing interest in trying to harness the arts and culture to goals of social regeneration and neighbourhood renewal.

This interest in culture as a social development tool was not entirely without precedent. As early as the 1980s, a policy of using arts for community development and empowerment was being pursued by the then Avon County Council, through its Department for Community Leisure. In an embryonic version of the philosophy of holistic, 'joined-up' government that was later to become the mantra of the New Labour government, Avon's community arts policy involved using community workers, youth workers and libraries in arts projects in disadvantaged neighbourhoods throughout the county. The abolition of Avon in the 1996 reorganisation of local government was a significant setback for work of this kind. Despite campaigning by the network of community-based arts sector workers that had developed, it was not possible to secure the same level of funding for local arts projects in the new unitary authority set-up.

Nevertheless, there were a number of projects that were continuing to do innovative work to secure social benefits through participation in arts activity. One of the most widely admired examples has been Hartcliffe School. Located in a disadvantaged estate on the southern periphery of the city, the school has pioneered an approach to raising the self-confidence and educational attainment of pupils by offering them the chance to take part in a range of arts-based projects, involving dancers, musicians and other personnel from leading companies. There are indications from research carried out in the school that participation in such extra-curricular activities has not only improved pupils' expressive and artistic skills, but has also led to better exam performance and improved perceptions of the locality (Kelly and Kelly, 2000, p 28). Another example is the community theatre company, ACTA, which describes itself as a company of facilitators, not a company of actors. Its core activity is work with communities to enable them to put on their own plays. The community in question might be geographical (such as a council estate), or a community that has something else in common (such as a learning-difficulty community). The thinking on which the company's work is based is that everyone has creative potential as well as a right to participate in arts activity, and participation in the arts can produce a range of social benefits. It can, for example, help to break down barriers of mistrust and misunderstanding between different sections of the population, especially between youth and older people. It can also lead to gains in self-confidence and self-esteem that may be enough to enable people to make modest, but significant, changes in their lives, such as getting a job, or breaking clear of drug dependency. The validity of these assumptions has been supported by the findings of extensive questionnaire surveys that ACTA has undertaken of former participants in its projects (Kelly and Kelly, 2000; Beddow, 2001).

Although local government reorganisation in 1996 caused some disruption to the funding of community-based arts projects, this has been more than offset by the opening up of a number of new funding sources during the latter half of the 1990s. These include the National Lottery and a variety of area-based, community regeneration programmes. ACTA is probably Bristol's leading example of an arts organisation that has succeeded in weaving together different sources of funding (National Lottery, council, and regeneration, for example) for projects that use creative activities for individual and community development in areas of high social stress. Its project, *Making a difference*, for example, worked with residents in four council estates to write and perform plays using funds from the National Lottery Charities Board. On the urban policy front, the 1998 Single Regeneration Budget allocation to the city (SRB4) included what is probably the city's most significant regeneration-funded arts project to date, the Knowle West Media Project, providing opportunities for young people in one of the city's most disadvantaged communities to participate in digital arts. In contrast to Bristol's other regeneration schemes, SRB4 has been thematic rather than geographical in orientation. Entitled YOUR (Youth Owning Urban Regeneration), its focus has been on

involving young people in finding solutions to youth issues in different areas of the city, a focus which has involved a variety of arts-oriented activities (Kimberlee et al, 2000).

The New Deal for Communities (NDC) scheme for Barton Hill is another recent example of the linking of arts to neighbourhood renewal. In keeping with the 'community-led' philosophy of the NDC programme as a whole, the main features of the Barton Hill scheme were put together over the course of a series of local meetings involving local artists and culture sector workers. Of the eight specified 'outcome areas' that were eventually identified, the arts and sport were included alongside other more familiar priorities such as tackling crime and raising educational attainment. The stated goal of the arts strand was to bring about an "increase in numbers of local residents involved in an artistic project" (Community at Heart, 1999, p 101). The rationale was that participation in the arts was a worthy regeneration goal in its own right, and not solely an instrument to achieve some other, non-artistic, end. In this respect, the NDC scheme appears to represent a new departure for area-based regeneration, at least in the Bristol context.

In addition to the NDC scheme at Barton Hill, arts and cultural action have been important elements in other area-based schemes in the city, such as the Education Action Zone (EAZ). These developments illustrate a growing awareness of the role that cultural activity can potentially play in the regeneration of disadvantaged neighbourhoods. It is evident, however, that the inclusion of artistic activities in neighbourhood renewal schemes can pose difficult challenges for (and to) prevailing administrative and bureaucratic processes. It is certainly too early to draw firm conclusions on the wider impacts of these initiatives.

Capital of culture?

As we have seen, from relatively small beginnings Bristol's cultural profile and strategy have expanded rapidly over the past decade or so. It is indicative of the city's confidence in its cultural assets and policy-making abilities that it embarked on a serious attempt to become European Capital of Culture in 2008 (one UK city is designated to receive the title in that year).

Designation as European Capital of Culture has proved a popular ambition for cities across Europe, providing the chosen city with opportunities for developing and consolidating its local culture, raising its international profile, attracting income from visitors and attention from potential investors. The experience of Glasgow as European City of Culture in 1990 was particularly influential in pointing towards the immediate cultural and economic benefits that could accrue. On the other hand, Glasgow's experience also pointed to some of the problems that could be encountered by stereotyping local culture, concealing local differences behind marketing hype, and alienating some sections of the local population. Although evaluating the longer-term impacts has proved difficult, there is nevertheless evidence of lasting benefits to chosen cities in terms of self-confidence, image and cultural tourism.

Bristol's decision to try for this cultural prize followed much prodding by business leaders and the director of the Cultural Development Partnership. The bid itself was prepared by the BCDP for submission in March 2002, and involved what it described as "the largest ever consultation exercise in the city".

Contrary to the expectations of many, Bristol was successful in being short-listed, from 12 candidates, alongside five other cities: Liverpool, Newcastle/ Gateshead, Birmingham, Cardiff and Oxford. Although it did not ultimately win the nomination, Bristol, together with the other unsuccessful short-listed cities, will be able to designate itself a centre of cultural excellence. The city's participation in the Capital of Culture competition has undoubtedly helped to raise the profile of the city and its cultural attributes. It has also been instrumental in securing progress on a number of new infrastructure projects, notably a new arena venue for pop concerts and other large-scale events. It is possible to advance several possible reasons for Bristol's failure to gain the main title. Despite the progress on the cultural policy front, it was less successful than other candidates in connecting the bid to a broader cultural strategy. Its need for the economic and image boost to be gained from the title was less pressing than that of Liverpool (the winning bid) and some other candidates. There was also a difficulty in coming up with a clear focus or decisive selling point, reflected in the criticisms raised publicly in the city that early versions of the

bid document were too bland and unimaginative. This is perhaps illustrative of a more long-standing ambiguity in the city over the cultural identity it wishes to project. Following failure to secure the title, however, those involved in the bid have nevertheless declared their objective of pressing ahead with the plans. This offers the possibility that the bidding process will prove to be a significant catalyst for change in practical terms.

Competition, cohesion and culture

Bristol has expanded its cultural profile and assets considerably since 1990. This is partly to catch up with other cities from a low level of activity in the early 1990s, but there is also evidence of recent rapid advance. How do these developments relate to the key issues of city competition and cohesion?

The relationship between culture and competition can be considered at a number of levels. First, there is the question of the competitiveness of Bristol's cultural industries relative to other cities. Here, there is evidence that particular types of television production and film making have prospered in the city. Animation and wildlife film-making production companies have been successfully competing in international markets and the city is well known to be the home of experts in these specialist fields. As a consequence, a specialist local labour market has grown up that underpins on-going success and the creation of new businesses. However, the overall impact is still relatively minor in terms of employment, and ultimately success in such domains can be quite fragile depending on rapid changes in markets, technology and regulation. Also, it is interesting to note that although these businesses are clustered in particular parts of the city, unlike in other cities such as Manchester, there has been little official attempt to create a more developed cultural quarter for these businesses, even though spatial clustering, innovation and mutual learning seem to be important in such industries. This is an issue that perhaps needs further analysis.

Second, there is the question of the relationship between successful cultural industries and the rest of the local economy within which they are embedded. The spin-off impacts are extremely difficult to measure given the volatility of some of these industries, but there is little evidence of particularly strong inter-linkages to other industries in the city, as opposed to linkages with businesses in other parts of the country. However, this is another issue that needs further analysis.

Third, there is the argument that cultural activity makes a city more competitive in terms of generating a positive image that both attracts and retains economic activity and wealth. Here the new Millennium projects have led the way in revitalising the city centre and acting as catalysts for large-scale, urban redevelopment and cultural tourism. Cultural infrastructures have thus certainly contributed to the on-going repopulation of the city centre, and the explosion of bars, nightclubs and restaurants. Although probably not crucial determinants, cultural facilities have also helped firms to retain and attract staff, and local universities to recruit a large and fairly affluent student population whose spending has fuelled further cultural activities.

The relationship between culture and social cohesion is more elusive. Within a city, cohesion can form around many different cores, such as family and kinship, neighbourhood, civic identity, class, and so on. As we saw earlier, increasing attention has been paid since the mid-1990s to participation in the arts as a vehicle for strengthening social ties and communal loyalties at the neighbourhood level, and overcoming mistrust and antagonism across the divides of age and ability. The Bristol experience also casts some light on the relationship between culture and cohesion at the civic, city-wide level. One of the major aspirations behind the cultural investment programme on Harbourside was that it might help to bring about a more socially inclusive city centre, to which all sections of the population might feel a sense of ownership and attachment. The loss of the proposed performing arts centre, the CPA, was a major blow to this strategy. More recently, the dockside area has become strongly associated with a rowdy, drinking and clubbing culture dominated by 18- to 25-year-olds, thereby undermining its role as a shared civic space, at least at night time. The designs for the Canons Marsh site have also provoked criticisms that the planned commercial elements, including bars and a multiplex cinema, will have the effect of reinforcing, rather than counteracting, the narrow social range of night-time visitors to the area. This is another area of possible conflict in cultural

strategies that warrants further analysis. Overall, however, our conclusion must be a positive one. Although progress has been uneven, cultural policies have become more varied and inclusive, and the range of cultural activities available in Bristol has grown considerably.

Social exclusion and the polarised city

Martin Boddy

The concept of social exclusion is now common currency in both academic research and policy discourse. Like many such terms, however, it has acquired multiple and overlapping meanings. Nevertheless, it provides an important focus for taking forward thinking from what might previously have been labelled 'poverty' and 'deprivation'. With the advent of the New Labour government elected under Tony Blair in 1997, the idea of social exclusion also increasingly informed the development of policy on the ground. The government was quick to establish the Social Exclusion Unit (SEU) within the Cabinet Office to address the fact that

> Over the past twenty years hundreds of poor neighbourhoods have seen their basic quality of life become increasingly detached from the rest of society. (SEU, 2001a, p 7)

It underpinned the government's overall 'welfare-to-work' strategy and has informed a wide range of policy initiatives including the work of the Neighbourhood Renewal Unit.

It is commonly suggested that the term 'social exclusion' originated in continental Europe: in France it was used to refer to those who did not fall within the state social insurance scheme (Lenoir, 1974), and was later extended to emphasise unemployment (Paugham, 1993, referred to in Burchardt et al, 1999). It gained wider currency in discussions of social policy around the European Community with some suggesting it perhaps represented a more palatable alternative to 'poverty'. In the UK context, some have argued, similarly, that social exclusion represents simply a re-labelling of the less fashionable concepts of poverty and deprivation

(Levitas, 1996, 1998). Others have distinguished between poverty, defined more narrowly as lack of money or material possessions, and the broader concept of social exclusion, the latter suggesting that individuals are in some way cut off from active engagement with some dimension(s) of 'normal society' (Atkinson, 1998; Burchardt et al, 1999).

Giddens, for example, writing in *The third way* (1998, p 104) argues that: "Exclusion is not about graduations of inequality, but about mechanisms that act to detach groups of people from the social mainstream". Social exclusion thus goes beyond the purely descriptive and captures notions of process or causal mechanisms. In similar fashion, Berghman (1995) sees social exclusion as a dynamic process rather than a state or outcome. This focuses attention on the idea that there are active *processes* or *mechanisms of exclusion* which in turn generate *outcomes* in terms of poverty and deprivation. This emphasises the need to focus on "the factors and processes by which people find themselves unable to participate in society and the economy or are cut off from the life chances available to the mainstream of society" (Hills, 1999, p 5).

Hills (1999, pp 5-6), building on Atkinson (1998) and Burchardt (1999), stresses five aspects of social exclusion:

Relativity: people are excluded from a particular society, as opposed to a focus on ability to purchase an 'absolute' basket of goods....

Multi-dimensionality: income and consumption are central, but so are other aspects of participation such as ability to carry out socially valued activity (not just paid work), political involvement and social interaction....

Agency: someone or something or some process is responsible for exclusion or inclusion occurring, while inability to control major aspects of one's life is an important aspect of being excluded.

Dynamics: such processes occur over time with long-lasting or cumulative effects. Duration in particular states matters and so do prospects for the future.

Multi-layered: exclusion operates at different levels — individual, household, community/neighbourhood, institutions.

While emphasising the importance of process and causal mechanisms, empirical research, seeking to operationalise ideas of social exclusion, has focused on what can be seen as the outcomes of processes of social exclusion. The outcomes of social exclusion are identified in terms of observable patterns of unemployment, health, school performance, and so on. Typically, individual indicators have been combined in more comprehensive attempts to map out different dimensions of exclusion. Howarth et al (1999) set out some 50 indicators as a basis for monitoring progress across a wide range of social and economic dimensions — referring to these as indicators of 'poverty and exclusion'. The government's then Department of the Environment, Transport and the Regions commissioned work to draw up 'indices of deprivation' drawing on a wide range of information sources, extending earlier indices based on population census data (DETR, 2000c). These new indicators have been widely used in a policy context as a basis for identifying geographical concentrations of deprivation (for example, DETR, 2000a) and have been made widely available both as individual indicators and combined in an overall index of deprivation (National Statistics, 2000).

Other empirical work has drawn on a number of UK survey-based data sets to develop comprehensive analyses of the outcomes of exclusion. Studies have typically sought to identify and to measure different dimensions of exclusion, captured by different sets of indicators. The 1999 Poverty and Social Exclusion Survey, for example, which followed up a sub-sample of the UK General Household Survey, explored four

dimensions of exclusion: exclusion from the labour market; exclusion from services; exclusion from social relations; and, finally, exclusion from adequate income or resources (poverty of impoverishment as such) (Gordon et al, 2000).

An influential set of studies has drawn on longitudinal and cohort-based surveys to examine different dimensions and causes of exclusion over time (Hobcraft, 1998, 2000; Machin, 1998; Burchardt et al, 1999; Hills, 1999; Sparkes, 1999). Burchardt et al (1999) use the British Household Panel Survey to measure social exclusion over the period 1991-95. They define social exclusion on the basis that

An individual is socially excluded if (a) he or she is geographically resident in a society and (b) he or she does not participate in the normal activities of citizens in that society. (Burchardt et al, 1999, p 230)

They then identify five more detailed dimensions of exclusion that they use as the basis for operating social exclusion in terms of different variables in the survey data. In similar fashion to Gordon et al (2000), they identify:

Consumption activity: being able to consume at least up to some minimum level of the goods and services that are considered normal for the society....

Savings activity: accumulated savings, pension entitlements, or owning property....

Production activity: engaging in an economically or socially valued activity such as paid work, education or training, retirement over state pension age, or looking after a family....

Political activity: engaging in some collective effort to improve or protect the immediate or wider social or physical environment....

Social activity: engaging in significant social interaction with family or friends and identifying with a cultural group or community.... (Burchardt et al, 1999, p 230)

Importantly, these studies have also started to look at different facets of the dynamics of exclusion. They have examined the extent to which exclusion at the individual level persists over time or is more transitory, relating exclusion in adult life to childhood contexts and experiences of exclusion, and looking at intergenerational patterns of exclusion.

This work suggests that for a proportion of individuals or households, exclusion is a temporary state, but that for the great majority it is persistent over time (Hills, 1999). Intergenerational mobility in terms of earnings and education is found to be limited (Machin, 1998). There are also strong links between social exclusion in adulthood and childhood experiences, which are important factors in maintaining such immobility. Hobcraft (1998, 2000) has shown that childhood poverty, family disruption, contact with the police and educational test scores are powerful predictors of social exclusion later in life. Educational qualifications show a clear and strong relationship with a wide range of measures of adult disadvantage at the age of 23 and 33. Childhood poverty has particularly strong effects, being the clearest predictor of negative adult outcomes even controlling for other factors. Indeed, Hobcraft (2000, p 34) refers to "the pervasive legacy of childhood poverty in later life". This work has identified in some detail the outcomes of social exclusion and starts to point to some of the processes driving exclusionary outcomes. It also has important implications for policy (Hills, 1999).

Social exclusion in the Bristol city-region

Having addressed broader debates around poverty and social exclusion, the rest of this chapter focuses on patterns and processes of social exclusion and polarisation in the Bristol city-region. The Bristol study provides the opportunity to examine these issues in the context of what is a relatively prosperous city-region. However, as already indicated in Chapter 2, Bristol, nevertheless, is a city-region marked by persistent concentrations of poverty, deprivation and polarisation across parts of the city-region itself. This section draws largely on the indicators of deprivation published by the Department of the Environment, Transport and the Regions in 2000 and available via National Statistics in order to operationalise the concept of social exclusion in Bristol. In this sense, it looks essentially at the outcomes of exclusion, but situates these in the

context of work referred to earlier in this chapter that attempts to identify underlying mechanisms.

Published indicators provide both an overall composite index of multiple deprivation and indicators for a number of different domains, including income, employment and health, each of which is in turn based on a number of components. The data provide a very detailed picture of deprivation down to ward level across the country as a whole. This provides the basis for a detailed picture of different aspects of deprivation across the Bristol city-region as a whole. It also allows the benchmarking of Bristol and neighbourhoods within it against the national picture.

Looking first at local authority district level, the City of Bristol was ranked 94th out of 354 districts locally on the overall index of multiple deprivation – where 1st represents the worst score – putting it almost in the worst quarter of districts as a whole (Table 6.1). Overall scores for the three surrounding districts were markedly higher, ranging from 229th in North Somerset to 299th out of 354 in South Gloucestershire. There is thus a clearly a marked contrast between Bristol and the surrounding districts.

This overall ranking reflects the full range of ward scores, both high and low. An alternative 'index of concentration' indicates the extent to which deprivation is concentrated in the worst wards rather than spread across the district as a whole (Table 6.1). This suggests that deprivation in Bristol and particularly North Somerset is rather more concentrated in particular parts of the respective districts than the overall average for ward scores would suggest. In Bristol, this seems to reflect the concentration of deprivation in the core inner-city wards and the outer estates. In the case of North Somerset, it is likely to reflect the geographical concentration of deprivation in particular rural areas.

Indicators of income deprivation and employment deprivation refer to specific domains within the overall index of multiple deprivation. As shown here (Table 6.1), they refer to rank based on absolute numbers rather than percentage scores. Larger districts, other things being equal, will tend to have larger absolute numbers of people income or employment deprived. Absolute rankings represent a

Table 6.1: DTLR index of multiple deprivation (2000), ranking of districts within Avon area out of 354 districts nationally (1 = worst)

	Rank of average of ward scores index of multiple deprivation	Rank of local concentration index of multiple deprivation	Rank of numbers income deprived	Rank of numbers employment deprived
Bath and North East Somerset	261	244	121	143
City of Bristol	94	71	13	13
North Somerset	229	107	105	111
South Gloucestershire	299	297	104	120

Source: National Statistics, Neighbourhood Statistics

Notes: Districts are ranked out of 354 districts nationally, where 1 = worst. Districts are ranked on the basis of their ward scores on the different indicators, weighted by population. The rank of average scores will reflect extreme scores, both high and low. Local concentration indicates the weighted average rank of a district's most deprived wards (those that contain 10% of the district's population). Income and employment scales represent absolute numbers of people deprived on these indicators, and therefore indicate the absolute scale of deprivation rather than a rate.

different but equally valid perspective on the scale of an issue such as income deprivation locally.

As a relatively large district in terms of national rankings, Bristol comes out 13th worst in terms of income and employment deprivation. The surrounding districts also look significantly worse in terms of absolute numbers income or employment

deprived than they do on the overall index of multiple deprivation.

Turning to the neighbourhood level, ward-based figures across the Avon area as a whole show the largest concentration of wards with high levels of multiple deprivation concentrated in the City of Bristol (Figure 6.1). Wards outside of Bristol do not

Figure 6.1: Index of multiple deprivation, Avon area (2000)

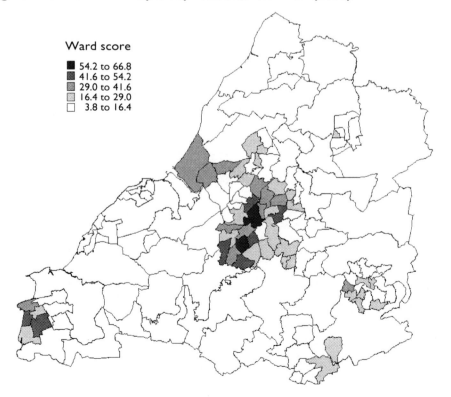

Ward score
- 54.2 to 66.8
- 41.6 to 54.2
- 29.0 to 41.6
- 16.4 to 29.0
- 3.8 to 16.4

Source: Joint Strategic Transport and Planning Unit (Bristol), from National Statistics, Neighbourhood Statistics

generally suffer the same intensity of deprivation seen inside Bristol. There are, however, three clusters of wards with levels of deprivation significantly higher than generally prevailing levels in the surrounding districts. These include a small number of wards in the urban centres of Weston-super-Mare and Bath and in the smaller towns of Norton Radstock/ Midsomer Norton in the relatively isolated former North Somerset coalfield area.

Within the City of Bristol itself, ward-level rankings give a detailed picture of the pattern and extent of

deprivation (Table 6.2). Rankings in terms of the overall index of multiple deprivation show that Bristol actually has five wards in the worst 10% of wards nationally: Ashley and Lawrence Hill in the core inner city; Filwood and Knowle on the southern fringe of the urban area, and Southmead to the north, covering outer estates of largely local authority housing. Lawrence Hill in the core inner city is 133rd out of 8,414 wards nationally and Filwood 221st. At the neighbourhood level, Bristol thus displays very significant levels of deprivation by national standards both in the core inner city and

Table 6.2: DTLR index of multiple deprivation and domain indices (2000), ranking of wards within the City of Bristol out of 8,414 wards nationally (1 = worst)

	Multiple deprivation	Income	Employ- ment	Health	Education	Housing	Access	Child poverty
Ashley	756	620	550	1,376	1,469	800	7,701	491
Avonmouth	1,955	2,199	2,718	1,993	746	2,281	6,224	2,301
Bedminster	2,951	3,532	3,481	3,327	582	4,706	7,282	3,616
Bishopston	6,897	5,797	5,375	6,340	6,775	3,361	7,804	6,217
Bishopsworth	935	1,328	1,917	1,635	51	1,169	5,770	1,349
Brislington East	3,040	2,567	3,731	3,522	1,777	2,609	6,001	2,647
Brislington West	4,485	4,287	5,138	5,206	1,815	3,432	6,878	4,502
Cabot	3,970	4,002	2,582	3,449	6,736	2,078	7,476	2,463
Clifton	7,172	6,435	4,887	6,790	7,775	3,606	7,438	6,353
Cotham	7,295	6,776	5,721	6,713	8,112	2,135	8,072	6,834
Easton	1,043	1,007	1,708	2,265	361	532	7,495	1,289
Eastville	1,998	2,215	2,788	2,701	798	1,840	4,794	2,495
Filwood	221	258	673	521	7	433	6,624	352
Frome Vale	2,765	2,415	2,874	1,741	2,503	5,346	5,442	2,961
Hartcliffe	1,036	1,808	1,705	1,500	56	1,627	6,064	1,593
Henbury	1,423	1,369	2,022	1,093	656	3,366	6,105	1,538
Hengrove	3,911	4,085	4,782	3,398	1,519	5,069	5,182	4,164
Henleaze	8,065	7,286	6,240	5,532	8,250	7,040	6,795	8,308
Hillfields	1,596	1,935	2,857	1,964	382	1,329	6,296	1,807
Horfield	2,504	2,530	3,012	2,259	1,211	3,381	6,448	2,213
Kingsweston	1,207	865	1,191	937	2,552	1,871	5,504	899
Knowle	733	1,006	1,584	1,393	83	688	5,554	1,189
Lawrence Hill	133	108	143	294	439	735	7,893	115
Lockleaze	1,095	720	1,929	1,607	647	1,536	5,383	734
Redland	7,367	7,055	5,171	6,592	8,200	3,160	7,145	7,874
Southmead	628	548	1,558	1,302	101	957	6,617	614
Southville	2,496	2,654	2,724	2,637	1,086	2,751	8,208	3,386
St George East	3,168	3,375	4,414	3,972	846	2,762	6,249	3,770
St George West	1,783	2,030	2,581	2,184	508	2,241	5,899	2,364
Stockwood	3,713	3,594	3,821	3,413	2,691	3,399	5,302	3,884
Stoke Bishop	5,819	5,640	5,164	6,377	3,210	5,203	4,690	4,310
Westbury-on-Trym	7,363	5,721	6,006	5,335	7,394	7,347	5,715	7,770
Whitchurch Park	921	1,059	1,226	1,329	378	997	6,977	820
Windmill Hill	1,278	1,809	1,856	1,989	234	1,077	7,163	1,823

Notes: Multiple deprivation is a composite index based on weighted scores of six of the individual domains (excluding child poverty which is a sub-index of the income domain, for children under 16). Each of the six domains is a composite index combining a range of variables.
Source: National Statistics, Neighbourhood Statistics

outer estates. There is also a high degree of polarisation between wards in Bristol reflected in very marked differences in ranking over short distances within the city. Southmead ward (ranked 628th nationally) sits next to Westbury-on-Trym (7,363th), and Ashley (756th) alongside Redland (7,367th).

Other more detailed issues are also evident. Ashley and Lawrence Hill in the core inner-city area, for example, are even worse in their ranking on employment deprivation than on multiple deprivation. The outer estates of Southmead, Knowle and Filwood, on the other hand, are more favourably ranked on employment than on multiple deprivation. This suggests that the nature of the problem does vary significantly between different neighbourhoods.

In overall terms, however, there is little to choose between the worst area in the core inner city and the worst area in the outer estates in terms of the severity of deprivation. This is despite clear contrasts in terms of housing type, for example, and tenure and social structure including ethnic mix. Thus, Lawrence Hill in the core urban area is ranked worst out of all the wards in Bristol on the index of multiple deprivation and four of the six sub-sets of indicators. Filwood in outer south Bristol is ranked second worst on the index of multiple deprivation and worst or second worst on five of the six sub-sets of indicators.

Polarisation

There is evidence, nationally, of increasing polarisation and a worsening of a range of indicators of social exclusion, against an overall background of continuing economic growth. There is evidence of increasing polarisation in terms of household incomes at the national level in the 1980s and 1990s. Net incomes of the lowest earning 10% of households fell by 8% between 1979 and 1994/95; net incomes of the best-off 10% rose by 68% (Hills, 1998). Households on less than 40% of the average rose from 7.3 million to 8.4 million between 1995 and 1998 (Howarth et al, 1999).

There is some evidence as well of an increasing polarisation within urban areas in terms of shares of unemployment between the best and worst wards; that is, a steepening of the curve from highest to

lowest. The Joseph Rowntree Foundation inquiry into income and wealth (1995) found that the already wide gap between the best and worst wards within urban areas had widened between the 1981 and 1991 Censuses of Population. This is borne out by a range of local studies (Pacione, 1997; Sheffield City Council, 1997).

In the case of Bristol, there is also some evidence of increasing polarisation with the worst wards accounting for an increasing share of unemployment. Yet the picture is complex. Discontinuities in data and boundaries make longitudinal analysis difficult. Over the period 1981-91, however, the three inner-city wards with the highest unemployment rates in 1981 (ranging from 16% to 22%) increased their share of total unemployment within the City of Bristol by 15%. Over the five-year period 1991-96, the share of total unemployment accounted for by these three inner-city wards changed little. (In fact, it actually fell slightly in St Pauls, the worst-off of the three).

Over the earlier period, 1981-91, the share of unemployment accounted for by the three outer estates with the highest levels of unemployment in 1991 (ranging from 11% to 15%) actually decreased their share of total unemployment by 20%. Their share of total unemployment continued to decline over the period 1991-96 by a further 16%.

The situation in the core inner-city wards thus deteriorated in the 1980s but appears to have stabilised in the 1990s. Over the same period, there has been a significant improvement in the situation of the outer-estate wards in the context of the city as a whole and particularly in relation to the core inner-city wards. South Bristol in particular has improved relative to the core inner city.

More generally at national level, a monitor of 50 different indicators of poverty and deprivation carried out for the Joseph Rowntree Foundation has found that, although 15 have improved, most have either remained unchanged or deteriorated in recent years, despite (modest) continuing year or year economic growth in the UK (Howarth et al, 1999). Even though unemployment has continued to fall, numbers of long-term workless households have remained continuously at over two million since 1995. In terms of health, the long-term sick rose from 3 million to 3.6 million between 1991 and 1998. And local government districts, where mortality rates were more than 10% above the average, increased from 28% in 1991 to 39% by 1998 (Howarth et al, 1999).

There is growing evidence as well, as suggested by figures on household income quoted earlier, that children particularly suffer disproportionately from social exclusion (Robson et al, 2000b). Deterioration in household incomes among the poor impacted on children – the proportion of all children growing up in households with less than half the average income grew from 10% in 1979 to 32% by 1994-95.

Income support beneficiaries are also proportionately more concentrated among families with children than among the population as a whole. Child poverty has continued to become more polarised, with high levels of poverty strikingly concentrated in the more urban areas. This suggests that social deprivation has impacted most severely on families with young children in the larger urban areas and that it is the young who have suffered most severely from social exclusion.

Other studies suggest that the concentration of deprivation in particular neighbourhoods is driven in part by allocation processes within the social housing sector and by the selective nature of these processes which concentrate particular types of tenants and households on particular estates (Brennan et al, 2000). This has been compounded by shrinkage of the sector under 'right-to-buy' legislation that has left 'residualised' less-popular estates, including 'outer estates', as a major part of the remaining stock. As Dickens et al (2000) remark, however, "the intensity of deprivation remains astounding". The role of social housing allocation processes would seem to be a dominant factor in the case of outer estates, consisting largely of socially rented housing. In geographical inner-city areas, selectivity operating within the private rented sector will tend to reinforce such processes.

It is sometimes argued that the concentration of worklessness and deprivation itself contributes to the problems of individuals and households, that living in such areas adds to levels of worklessness and deprivation and makes it harder to escape from them (Hills, 1999). This could be due to employers

discriminating consciously or unconsciously against job seekers from such areas, since local residents lack well-developed contacts or networks linking them to possible job opportunities, or because there are fewer jobs available locally. Buck (2001) found that 'neighbourhood effects' could have some impact but were relatively weak compared with the more powerful effects of the characteristics and background of individuals and households. In a review of the evidence, Kleinman (1998) suggested that neighbourhood effects were weak and tended to be proxies for other factors. Recent empirical work by Brennan et al (2000), however, has made a strong argument that multiple factors combine to produce significant additional disadvantage stemming from particular neighbourhoods. This, they argue, provides a powerful argument for comprehensive area-based initiatives.

Education and social exclusion

A key factor in the cumulative, multi-factor process of neighbourhood disadvantage identified by Brennan et al (2000) is educational attainment. As noted earlier, Hobcraft (2000) and others have pointed to the crucial importance of early childhood and educational attainment as a factor explaining social exclusion in later life. Low levels of educational attainment, and related social and life skills, are major sources of social exclusion, including later exclusion from the labour market and employment opportunities and a wide range of other indicators of exclusion (Machin, 1998; Sparkes, 1999; Hobcraft, 2000). This provides strong evidence that educational performance and school outcomes are to a significant degree affected by the social and economic characteristics of the neighbourhood in which individual schools are located. Issues of individual school performance and teaching quality highlighted by UK governments and their advisors in recent years can therefore only be a partial response to the evidence of educational under-performance in particular cities and neighbourhoods.

In terms of education, moreover, there is a particular and increasing concentration of children from poor households in particular under-performing schools (Robson et al, 2000b) (Table 6.3). It is also notable that performance appears to grow worse at later stages of schooling: the relative under-performance of

Table 6.3: Educational performance by settlement type (%)

Categories	Pupils aged 6 with <level 3 SAT (1998)	Pupils aged 10 with <level 4 SAT (1998)	Pupils aged 15 with no/low GCSEs (1997)
Inner London	21.8	11.3	8.8
Main metropolitan areas	19.3	10.0	10.9
Large cities	22.8	11.0	8.8
Other metropolitan areas	18.1	8.9	8.1
Industrial	17.8	8.7	6.3
Outer London	17.6	7.3	6.2
Small cities	20.1	9.7	7.9
New towns	17.3	7.7	5.9
Resort/retirement areas	17.5	7.5	5.2
Mixed urban/rural areas	14.4	5.8	3.9
Remote rural	15.4	6.7	4.0
ENGLAND	17.5	8.1	6.4
Conurbations			
Greater London (Inner London)	19.1 (21.8)	8.7 (11.3)	7.0 (8.8)
Greater Manchester (Manchester)	18.0 (23.0)	8.2 (10.8)	8.0 (14.6)
Merseyside (Liverpool)	16.1 (17.8)	7.9 (10. 3)	10.0 (12.5)
South Yorkshire (Sheffield)	19.5 (19.2)	10.6 (11.3)	10.2 (10.3)
Tyne and Wear (Newcastle-upon-Tyne)	18.1 (17.6)	8.8 (12.7)	9.6 (14.7)
West Midlands (Birmingham)	20.0 (20.3)	9.8 (10.1)	8.2 (9.5)
West Yorkshire (Leeds)	18.2 (17.2)	10.1 (7.6)	9.4 (9.3)
Cleveland (Middlesbrough)	17.5 (20.6)	8.9 (8.6)	8.4 (14.7)

Note: the core cities of the conurbations are shown in brackets.
Source: Robson et al (2000b)

urban areas becomes progressively poorer between ages six, 10 and 15 (Table 6.3). Further, there is a consistently worse performance in more urban areas and (with the sole exception of Leeds) within core cities as against the overall conurbations.

Looking at the Bristol city-region, there is clear evidence, again, of a marked degree of polarisation. There are significant differences in educational outcomes in the maintained sector within the Bristol city-region as a whole, with Bristol city falling significantly behind the other three unitary authorities and below national levels from Key Stage 2 through to A/AS Level and Advanced GNVQ (Table 6.4). Pupils in state sector schools in Bristol city generally perform well below the national average, and those from schools in the three surrounding districts considerably better than average. In 2002, only 66% of pupils in Bristol city gained Level 4 or above in Maths at Key Stage 2 compared with the national average of 73%, and 78% of pupils in Bath and North East Somerset. Only 31% of 15-year-olds in Bristol gained five or more A★-C grades

in GCSE/GNVQs compared with 52% nationally and 58% in Bath and North East Somerset.

Both Bristol, and Bath and North East Somerset also have a particularly high proportion of students in the independent sector. Twenty seven per cent of all students in Bristol were educated in the independent sector, and 22% of those aged 15+ (compared with less than 3% in North Somerset and South Gloucestershire in 2001). This is a further dimension of polarisation, given that educational outcomes vary greatly between the independent and state sectors. Some 91% of independent sector students in Bristol attained 5+ grade A★-C GCSE passes in 2001 compared with only 33% in the state sector in Bristol – well below the national average for the state sector of 50%. This is reflected in the mean scores per pupil between the two sectors (Table 6.5).

Similar contrasts in terms of performance between the independent and state sectors apply to A/AS level outcomes (Table 6.6).

Table 6.4: Education performance (2002), Key Stage 2 and GCSE/NVQ (%)

	Pupils gaining level 4+ Maths Key Stage 2 in maintained schools	15-year-olds gaining 5+ A*-C GCSE/GNVQ in maintained schools	Average capped point score in maintained schools	Mean GCSE/GNVQ score per 15-year-old in independent schools
Bath and North East Somerset	77.9	58.4	36.8	56.9
Bristol City	65.9	31.0	26.8	58.8
North Somerset	74.8	53.3	35.9	27.6
South Gloucestershire	75.8	52.4	35.9	–
England	73.0	51.6	34.7	52.5

Source: National Statistics, Department for Education and Science, *Performance Tables 2002: Key Stage 2 Test Results* and *Secondary School Performance Tables 2002*

Table 6.5: Secondary school performance in the maintained and independent sectors (2001)

	Mean GCSE/GNVQ score per 15-year-old in maintained schools (%)	Mean GCSE/GNVQ score per 15-year-old in independent schools (%)
Bath and North East Somerset	41.8	56.9
Bristol City	30.0	58.8
North Somerset	40.3	27.6
South Gloucestershire	39.4	–
England	39.3	52.5

Source: National Statistics, Department for Education and Skills, *2001 Secondary Schools Performance Tables*, and figures supplied by the Department for Education and Skills

At a more detailed level, patterns of concentration and polarisation are even more marked. No fewer than 16 of the city's 34 wards are ranked in the worst 10% of wards nationally in terms of education. Filwood is ranked 7th out of 8,414, making it one of the worst 10 wards in the country as a whole (see Table 6.2). The adjoining South Bristol wards of Bishopsworth, Hartcliffe and Knowle are in the worst 100 wards nationally and Southmead in the north of the city is ranked 101st. All five wards cover outer estates of mainly local authority housing.

This is a remarkable concentration of educational deprivation, measured by national standards within the generally prosperous City of Bristol. And the problem extends more generally across many parts of the city. On the other hand, there is marked polarisation evident as well, with three wards in the north-west sector of the city, Cotham, Henleaze and Redland, actually in the best 5% of wards nationally, and Clifton and Westbury-on-Trym not far behind.

The role of the social housing and private rented sectors in concentrating deprivation in certain neighbourhoods was noted earlier. The impacts of the educational system would seem, however, to play potentially a very important role in both driving and reinforcing spatial patterns of deprivation and

Table 6.6: Education performance, A/AS level and advanced GNVQ

	Mean score for 17-year-old A/AS Level and advanced GNVQ candidates in maintained schools, 2001	Mean score for 17-year-old A/AS Level and advanced GNVQ candidates in independent schools, 2000
Bath and North East Somerset	15.6	22.9
Bristol City	13.5	22.7
North Somerset	17.3	13.3
South Gloucestershire	16.5	20.5
England	17.3	24.0

Source: National Statistics, Department for Education and Skills, *2001 School and College (Post-16) Performance Tables*, and figures supplied to author by Department for Education and Skills

segregation. There would seem to be an important interaction between housing allocation processes and educational allocation processes (Butler and Robson, 2001).

It has not been possible in the work on Bristol to explore these factors in detail. Social–spatial polarisation in places more successful than Bristol would, however, seem to reflect this interaction of housing markets and bureaucratic systems of housing allocation on the one hand, and 'markets' for schooling on the other. Test results and exam performance in Bristol demonstrates increasing polarisation in the public education sector in terms of school performance. Patterns of outwards migration suggest that better-off households (that is, those able to move) have over recent years increasingly developed patterns of movement and residential preference that have exacerbated this. In the case of Bristol, this has involved patterns of movement within the City – avoiding the south of the City and favouring the north. It has also encouraged demand in areas of new greenfield development on or beyond the urban fringe in the surrounding districts, where school performance is in some cases spectacularly better. This pattern of residential preference is reinforced in terms of inwards migration from outside of the city-region. It is further exacerbated in the case of Bristol by the high proportion of children who are educated in the city's large private school sector – a legacy, in part, of endowments from the city's mercantile past. Many of those who can afford private education do so; those who cannot, but who can afford to move into the catchment areas of the better schools, do so; those who can do neither are stuck.

Conclusions

The concept of social exclusion usefully focuses on the processes and causal mechanisms that underlie empirical measurement of poverty and social exclusion. Recent work has emphasised the multiple and complex factors which interact in a cumulative fashion to generate spatially persistent concentrations of deprivation. Longitudinal studies have also demonstrated the persistence through time of poverty and deprivation for many individuals and households. They have also clearly demonstrated the persistent effects of the experience of poverty

deprivation and exclusion in childhood resulting in disadvantage later in life.

The case of Bristol shows very clearly the extent to which geographically concentrated disadvantage is characteristic of relatively prosperous city-regions in southern England. This is evident comparing the core urban area with the surrounding districts. It is particularly striking, however, at a more detailed neighbourhood level. Both the geographical inner-city and outer-social housing estates show marked concentrations of deprivation by national standards. As elsewhere, this is likely to reflect to a large extent the 'sorting' effects of the housing market. As Brennan et al (2000) argue, however, this process is likely to be reinforced by cumulative 'neighbourhood' effects that make worse the disadvantage suffered by individuals and households.

These mutually reinforcing effects reflect a combination of factors. Particularly important among these is educational performance. As Hobcraft (2000) and others emphasise, this is rooted in the social context of households and neighbourhoods with a low incidence of paid work and low levels of attachment to work and to education. The effects, moreover, are particularly long-lasting. Educational performance in Bristol city compares unfavourably both with the national average and with the surrounding districts in the city-region. Almost half of the city's wards fall in the worst 10% of wards nationally in terms of educational deprivation. Four are in the worst 100 wards nationally. This represents a remarkable concentration of educational deprivation by national standards in what is, overall, a generally prosperous city-region. It would seem clear that educational performance is a significant factor generating persistent poverty and deprivation both in the core inner city but also, particularly, the city's outer-social housing estates. It would also seem likely that out-migration by those households who can move, together with overall patterns of residential preference in favour of the catchment areas of the better performing schools, has reinforced these effects further. There is, thus, a powerful interaction between processes of 'educational sorting' and the sorting effects of the housing market as discussed earlier.

7

Towards collaborative capacity
Murray Stewart

Introduction

Urban policy over the past half century has been characterised by constant change in the nature, role and functioning of the institutions thought by government to be appropriate to manage urban change (DETR, 2000e). Bristol, as elsewhere, has experienced a succession of policy instruments, a fragmentation of institutions and a proliferation of initiatives as the traditional responsibilities and powers of the local authority have been diminished and dispersed. The city has been the recipient of a succession of special urban initiatives from the Traditional Urban Programme through Programme Authority status, through Task Force and Urban Development Corporation to Single Regeneration Budget (SRB) and New Deal for Communities (NDC). Much more importantly, however, have been a number of new territorial, fiscal and administrative regimes affecting the main programmes – two local government reorganisations, new forms of local taxation, competition and best value in service provision, and new political arrangements. This chapter looks at the culmination of this era of fragmentation and initiative proliferation, at the consequent emergence of new urban governance in Bristol, and at the prospects for the creation and exploitation of 'collaborative capacity'.

'Government' can be defined as the activity of the formal governmental system, conducted under clear procedural rules, involving statutory relationships between politicians, professionals and the public, taking place within specific territorial and administrative boundaries. It involves the exercise of powers and duties by formally elected or appointed bodies, and using public resources in a financially accountable way. 'Governance', on the other hand, is a much looser process often transcending geographical or administrative boundaries, conducted across public, private and voluntary/community sectors through networks and partnerships often ambiguous in their memberships, activities, relationships and accountabilities. It is a process of multi-stakeholder involvement, of multiple interest resolution, of compromise rather than confrontation, of negotiation rather than administrative fiat. Transaction costs are minimised, trust maximised, collaborative advantage extracted.

In principle, therefore, the new urban governance establishes shared objectives and common purpose, operates through inter-organisational bargaining and negotiation, pursues joint planning and delivery through shared resources, all based in a value system of mutual interest, trust and reciprocity. In practice, joint working is often characterised by the absence of such features and the history of joint working has been one of only limited success (Stewart et al, 1999; DETR, 2000a). There is a marked absence of sufficient collaborative capacity to draw together local stakeholders to act in a way that creates synergy.

Collaboration has been pursued most obviously through partnership working. There is now a wide literature on the nature and form of collaboration in general and partnership working in particular (De Groot, 1992; Mackintosh, 1993; Hastings, 1996; Skelcher et al, 1996; Skelcher and Lowndes, 1998; Huxham, 1996; Sullivan and Skelcher, 2002). For most new governmental initiatives, such working is a required form, representing a mandated or imperative coordination (Webb, 1991). Partnership working has also increasingly been dominated by procedural arrangements for bidding, delivery plan preparation, project appraisal, monitoring and performance review (following Webb's bureaucratic mode of coordination). Above all, however, partnership working reflects the network mode of governance that has characterised much writing about the new governance (Marsh and Rhodes, 1992). It is argued that it is through networking that collaborative capacity can be created and exploited.

The distinction has been widely made between market, hierarchy and network modes of governance. Once more, partnership working – which has strongly shaped the patterns of collaboration in Bristol as elsewhere – contains elements of all three modes. It is shaped by the market paradigm (since partnerships have been a required form for competing for resources and delivering outputs under contract) and by the hierarchy paradigm with both paradigms again reflecting Webb's mandated and bureaucratic modes.

This chapter, however, focuses primarily on the network paradigm as applied to urban governance. Drawing on a number of papers produced throughout the period of the ESRC Bristol Integrated City project (Stewart, 1998, 2000, 2002; Sweeting and Stewart, 1999), it reflects on the nature of the institutional arrangements which have characterised collaborative working in South West England in general and the Bristol city-region in particular over recent years. It links this empirical evidence from Bristol to a broader debate about the policy requirements for collaboration and coordination in urban policy, and, more pragmatically, to the recent emergence of Local Strategic Partnerships (LSPs) as the preferred policy machinery for addressing goals of urban competitiveness and cohesion (DETR, 2000d; DTLR, 2001a).

It is essential to place this most recent experience within a longer timescale, since relations between public, private and voluntary sectors are slow to change and history sets the context within which new forms of collaboration can emerge. The first part of this chapter, therefore, sets out the historical context for collaborative working in Bristol. The second describes in brief the features of the institutional map of the city-region, providing a description of the array of partnerships that have been established over recent years. The third part

relates this empirical base to a number of themes in the traditional literature of government and power – central–local relations and the role of the state, the changing forms of local democracy, and the emergence of coalitions and regimes. The fourth section focuses more explicitly on network governance, on the operation of the complex interlocking web of partnerships which has characterised the governance of Bristol, and on the forces which have (or, as we argue, have not) driven collaboration. The final part of this chapter draws out some of the implications for the future of urban governance and the role of LSPs.

The historical context

The history of Bristol has been one of long-standing independence and self-reliance (Dresser and Ollerenshaw, 1996). Over many decades, Bristol institutions have appeared to regard themselves as being above national debate (as illustrated by an unwillingness until the 1920s to adopt Greenwich as the basis for telling Bristol time, or by occasional absence of the city council from the Association of District Councils or of the Bristol Chamber of Commerce from the Association of British Chambers of Commerce). In 1974, therefore, the loss to the new County of Avon of both strategic planning and key service powers (education and social services) represented a severe blow to self-confidence. It resulted in 20 years of civic sulking about the relegation of the city to district council status and arguably reinforced an introspection that still characterises the governance of the city-region.

The Bristol economy has for centuries been a strong one since the days of the notorious triangular intercontinental trade, and the wealth generated from the translation of imported raw materials into finished manufactured goods for home consumption or export. Most recently, however, the 1980s saw recognition of the downturn of the Bristol economy, of the challenges to what had traditionally been an affluent and pleasant growth location, and of the increased polarisation between affluence and poverty (Boddy et al, 1986).

Private sector interest in governance was awakened; The Bristol Initiative (TBI) was formed. Established as a local force for change modelled on the

Confederation of British Industry's 'initiatives beyond charity' (CBI, 1988), TBI saw one main challenge as:

> ... being organised to manage change in a way which respects the duties and responsibilities of those democratically elected to look after the city yet offers a unified view of what is possible in the interests of the community as a whole. (TBI, 1989)

The Bristol Chamber of Commerce and Initiative (BCCI) – the first organisation to reflect a merger between a business leadership team on Confederation of British Industry lines and the local Chamber of Commerce – began to forge a single private sector view on Bristol issues. For many years, relations between public and private sectors in Bristol had been strained, notably in relation to business rate levels, parking and the (re)development of the central area with little constructive contact between local business and the council (Stewart, 1976). Development and conservation interests had often been confrontational (Punter, 1990). Through the late 1980s there had been little pressure for conciliation between public and private sectors (Stewart, 1986).

Unsurprisingly, the city council was at first suspicious of these new private sector moves but was willing to talk with TBI, and a number of new partnerships (for example, Bristol 96, Broadmead, Cultural Development) were instigated in the early 1990s. Nevertheless, some Labour councillors, as well as many managers and professionals within the city council, remained rooted in traditional attitudes. The ambivalence felt by some to partnerships – which were perceived to have been imposed by central government – was reflected in the bitterness of two City Challenge rejections in 1991 and 1992 (Malpass, 1994; Oatley and Lambert, 1995). One view after these setbacks was that partnerships brought no benefits. A senior Labour politician felt after the failures to win City Challenge that it would be "back to normal ... back to the City Council taking charge" (quoted in Malpass, 1994).

Indeed, throughout this period the council had anticipated the return to power of a Labour government. At the same time, there were those in the Chamber of Commerce, itself coming to terms with the unexpected impact which the second recession was having on two key regional sectors (defence and financial services), who considered that the new private sector engagement with civic matters was a diversion from the real business interests. Conservative victory in the 1992 General Election, however, marked a fundamental shift in political positions, and from mid-1992 the council altered its structures, staffing and much of its senior personnel. Traditionally highly departmentalised, the council began to develop a more corporate structure supported by a central policy unit. Traditional policies and practices were re-examined, and some radical decisions taken, not least the sale of the Port of Bristol. On the advent of Local Government Review, the city council sought the return of City and County status and pursued relatively non-confrontational policies until that was secure.

As a consequence, the period 1992-96 was characterised as a time of waiting for reorganisation, of mutual learning, of breaking down of stereotypes, of gradual movement into joint working, and of cautious exploration of the enabling style. A culture of inter-sectoral working was established (Snape and Stewart, 1996; Stewart, 1997b; Adburgham, 1998), with a few key leaders promoting the normative framework that enabled partnerships to occur (Sweeting and Stewart, 2001). What appears peculiar to Bristol, however, even at this early stage of the new governance, was the slow, indecisive, ambivalence surrounding changes in the nature of city governance. Despite helpful shifts in structures and relationships, there was arguably relative immobility in governmental capacity. The city council had historically been introspective, directing itself to service provision and the needs of its residents. Local imperviousness to external influence had long been the hallmark of Bristol conservatism. There was a legacy from the long-standing cliquishness in networks of governance (Miller, 1958a, 1958b), from the absence of the private sector from civic affairs, and latterly from the unwillingness in the early 1990s of the city council to act positively as it awaited the outcomes of local government reorganisation and the hoped for return of unitary status. It was a period, in effect, of partnership on probation. It was onto this context, following the advent of Labour government in 1997, that the 'new urban governance' was imposed, and it is with the response of the city-region to that imposition that the remainder of this chapter is concerned.

The changing institutional map of governance

The policies and programmes of the Labour government over the period from 1997 hastened changes in the regional institutional map from three directions. First, there came a revived regionalism, with a subsequent associated sub-regionalism, spawning institutional capacity building above and beyond the city-region. A range of regional institutions evolved, with an enhanced government office role, a new South West of England Regional Development Agency (SWERDA), and a regional assembly, all paralleled by the establishment of numerous advisory/consultative groups and the regionalisation of many other bodies within the non-departmental public body, and private and voluntary sectors. Sub-regional partnerships were also encouraged (Robson et al, 2000a).

Second, the government's insistence on better service delivery through joined-up service planning and delivery required a set of city-wide partnerships. Many of these were formed in response to statutory requirements but others developed as voluntary initiatives (often in the Bristol case through the impetus of the BCCI) in response to locally perceived needs and issues. The Bristol Regeneration Partnership (BRP, 2001) listed 17 city-wide partnerships in existence by mid-2001 including, for example, Regeneration, Cultural Development, Community Safety, Early Years, Agenda 21, Health, Housing, and Sport.

Third, there emerged in Bristol, as elsewhere, an array of small area-based initiatives (ABIs) concerned both with countering exclusion and with targeting resources into areas where main programmes of governance have failed. In the South West, Plymouth was the recipient of the full range of such ABIs, but Bristol, as a major focus for disadvantage and deprivation in the region, also gained a number of such initiatives, including, over a period, eight regeneration schemes arising from successive rounds of SRB funding, two Education Action Zones (EAZs), two Sure Start programmes, two EU URBAN programmes, an EU Objective 2 programme, and a NDC Pathfinder.

The institutional map (Figure 7.1) illustrates the complexity of this system of governance as it was in 1991. The consequence was that the city-region became institutionally crowded with both regional/sub-regional and neighbourhood/area-based structures pressing in on the more long-standing mechanisms for the government of the city. Relationships between many of the boxes were unstructured and unclear, but in addition many of the boxes in Figure 7.1 represent groupings or partnerships in themselves, each incorporating complex inter-organisational membership and relational and operational characteristics.

It is not the purpose of this chapter to describe the map in detail or indeed to defend its accuracy. Drawn in the early months of 2001, it has already become dated at all levels as regional, sub-regional and institutional governance structures have evolved, as modernisation has bitten on the systems of service planning and delivery at city level, and as new ABIs have continued to be established. Most notably the requirements for Neighbourhood Renewal and LSPs have changed some elements of the map. The function of the diagram, rather, is to illustrate the complexity of the administrative arrangements which have affected the city-region, and to highlight a number of issues inherent in the new governance.

Some of these issues are discussed in greater detail later in this chapter. First comes an observation of the continuing impact of central government in the region and city despite the rhetoric of devolution and decentralisation. The issue here is the role of the state in any new 'localism' and the extent to which central state practices dominate in the governance of the city-region. Following from this comes a second question about the relationship between state and civil society and the nature of local democracy under a complex system of governance such as that illustrated earlier in this chapter. Third comes the final question – what are the less visible structures of influence and power? If power does not lie democratically with the people, is it concentrated within less accountable groupings of interests – an urban coalition or regime?

Figure 7.1: ESRC 'Cities: Competition and Cohesion' programme (Bristol Integrated Study)

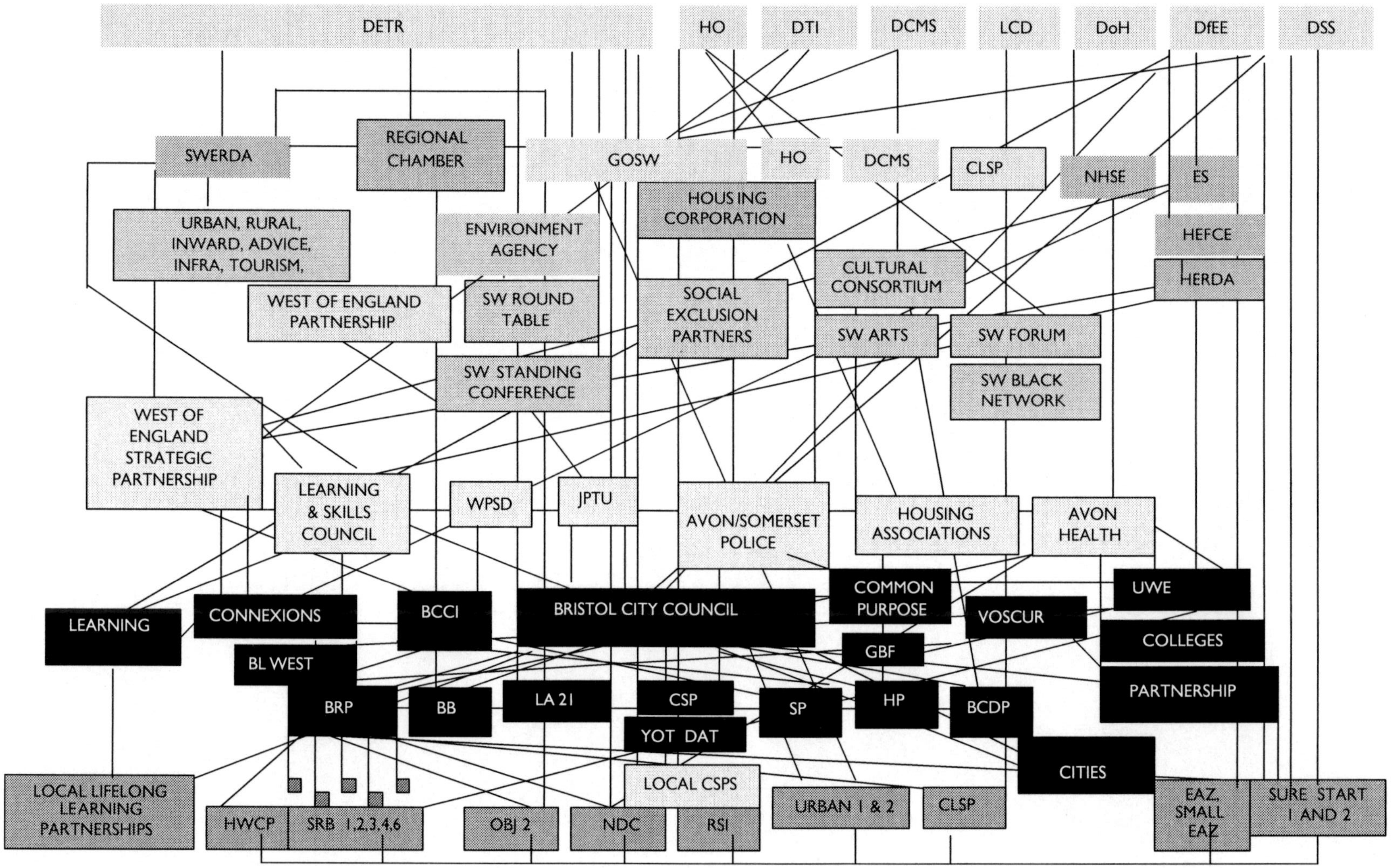

Institutional patterns and theories of government

Central–local relations and the role of the state

Vertical relationships have historically been strong and reflect the functional specialisation built into UK public administration for 80 years since the Haldane Report (Haldane, 1918). Horizontal relationships are those which operate territorially at regional and city levels. Conversely, they are relatively weak, reflecting the centralisation of the British state, the pre-eminence of the Westminster Parliament, and the dominance of the civil service. While, in principle, policy aims to devolve downwards to regions and local government, in practice, the centre (ministers and officials) retain tight control. This retention of influence by the centre confounds the hollowed state thesis, the argument (Rhodes, 1994; Jessop, 1995) that there is a shift of power upwards to Brussels, outwards to arm's-length agencies, and downwards to region and locality. Hollowing may be plausible in an upward direction, with the interests of the British nation state struggling to assert themselves in Europe. Downwards, however, the central state has moved to occupy the new regional space left vacant – indeed largely ignored – after the 1996 reorganisation of local government (Stewart, 1997a). This alleged shift of power, therefore, is more realistically recognised to involve a redistribution rather than loss of role and function, with many of the same functions exercised at different territorial levels, and in different organisational forms, but with little devolution of state power (Holliday, 2000; Taylor, 2000). Holliday argues that "the state may be to an extent fragmented but this does not mean it is disabled…. The British core is more substantial than ever before". The evidence suggests that Whitehall perceives it to be important that central government should capture, as opposed to merely occupy, the regional ground (Cabinet Office, 2000). The weakness of the Government Offices for the Regions is diagnosed as a failure of organisational culture which government has sought to rectify by demanding a louder and more articulate government voice in the regions. The establishment of the Regional Co-ordination Unit and its role in reviewing and integrating ABIs, and the enhancement of government office in terms of neighbourhood renewal and local strategic

partnerships is further evidence of continuing central presence.

Hence, there has been in the South West as in other regions the establishment of a new governmental presence. The consolidation in the regions of departments hitherto largely invisible at sub-national level – Culture, Media and Sport and the Home Office, for example – is one example, the creation of Regional Directors of Public Health another. There is clearly a displacement of governmental activity, but Deas and Ward (1999) see this less as hollowing out but rather as seepage from the central state. This seepage, moreover, is differentially 'licensed' as the various sub-national arms are accorded the right to plan and provide local services through a combination of market and bureaucratic mechanisms.

The South West institutional map shows how some central departments retain strong control over main programmes (for example education, health, policing and children). The centre also exercises influence through the establishment and, on occasion, active participation in, special initiatives (Sure Start, NDC and EAZs). Others link more closely to local authority structures or to the oversight (often benevolent) of larger partnerships. Nevertheless, where regional, sub-regional or local partnerships carry responsibility, central government is rarely an active partner, retaining an observer, 'friend at court' role, and reserving its position as arbiter of resource allocation. Latterly, the accreditation role afforded to government offices in relation to LSPs emphasised this adjudication role.

While the vertical linkages are strong, there is less evidence of horizontal integration. In the South West as elsewhere, restructuring of the government office has enhanced the integrative function, and senior office staff play an active role in facilitating and supporting local joint working. A matrix management system links territorial responsibilities with functional ones in the government office regional executive team, and new central government players – Home Office, Health, DCMS and MAFF (now DEFRA) – are being drawn into the regional team. The influence of the centre remains strong, however, and where there is competition between central government players (or between their agencies or programmes in the regions), central stakeholders can be seen to build alliances with local stakeholders in order to create a coalition of influence. The proactive response of the Government Office of the South West (GOSW) to the establishment of SWERDA through the creation of a regional Social Exclusion Partners' group was one illustration of this jockeying for position, the tenacity with which the Department of the Environment, Transport and the Regions (subsequently Department for Transport, Local Government and the Regions, now the Office of the Deputy Prime Minister) held onto NDC and the neighbourhood agenda (and indeed become actively engaged on the ground) another, the polarisation of roles between government offices and RDA a third.

Democracy and accountability

The continued presence of the centre in local affairs has implications for the relations between state and civil society, and once again Bristol reflects the ambiguity inherent in current moves to new governance. Three strands of change coexist and interact: the creation of an enhanced participative democracy; the rehabilitation of representative democracy; and the continuation of governance by quango and network.

The shift towards a more *participative* democracy places the emphasis on the engagement of local people in the management of their local affairs. In part, this is investment in "the vital resources of 'social capital' such as trust or community spirit being undermined by rapid turnover of people and increased fear of crime" (SEU, 2001). This implies the encouragement of more interactive social relations at local level, assistance for organisations and clubs, and mutual social support in circumstances of disadvantage and powerlessness. The application of this philosophy is most evident in the range of ABIs in general, and in neighbourhood-based working in particular. Bristol now has a considerable number of ABIs – the Barton Hill 'Community at Heart' NDC scheme, the SRB 5 Hartcliffe and Withywood Community Partnership, the Sure Start projects in Hartcliffe and in Knowle, two European URBAN projects, the St George EAZ and others (BRP, 2001). The creation of a more active participative democracy is also the aim of a number of the government's proposals for local government modernisation – Best Value, Community Planning,

electoral reform, leadership and restructuring of council business.

The city council has moved some way to recognise and respond to this more active civil society, towards decentralised forms of service planning and delivery and more extensive community consultation. The Agenda 21 processes (the foundation of the Community Strategy) derived from extended stakeholder involvement; there was very positive city council support for the NDC residents in building the NDC partnership; the Neighbourhood Renewal Strategy proposes new Neighbourhood Partnerships. All these reflect the centrality of democracy, inclusion and cohesion in the council's espoused core values, but also its adherence to the principles of *representative* democracy. The *Bristol democracy plan* (BCC, 1998), prepared before council reorganisation into executive and scrutiny, sought to make the council more accountable locally through the strengthening of councillor roles and capacity at ward level, and by decentralising to an area basis for a number of functions. An engaged population, voting in numbers, being consulted, being offered some forms of participative democracy would reflect a more engaged community, hence perhaps more cohesive (although, also more conflictual, perhaps). This greater inclusiveness in principle creates a stronger city – perhaps a more competitive one, and the formal representative system (the council) might benefit from a spin off from this greater involvement. Various initiatives in community engagement illustrate the point – Choices for Bristol, IRIS (Involving Residents in Solutions), Network South Bristol, On the Nail, Citizens' Panel and Agenda 21 consultation (the probable basis for Community Planning): all represent in different ways new approaches to community engagement. One strand, therefore, of the new governance in Bristol is an attempted rehabilitation of representative democracy, induced in part by legislation requiring local government reform and in part by a council wanting to re-engage its electorate and retain electoral support. This has only partially been successful, since the positive moves listed above were offset by poor publicity associated with the 2001 referendum on the budget, with the departure of the chief executive, and with a continued perception that the council is driven by self-interest rather than collective benefit. It was widely believed in 1991 that the then leadership of the council did not perceive the LSP to be to the council's advantage.

Therefore, there has been uncertainty surrounding the future directions of participative and representative democracy, together with recognition that there may be a tension between them. In the NDC board elections, community members were elected on a higher turnout than was achieved in the local council elections (held on General Election day); a resident declared "we are the councillors here now". This tension between participative and representative democracy is compounded by what was described as a crisis of accountability. Only a few of the boxes shown in the institutional map (Figure 7.1) have directly elected management – Bristol City Council, a number of the boards or management committees of voluntary organisations, some local partnerships, and the board of the Chamber of Commerce. Others have delegate representation – that is, nominated members both from elected bodies and/or health, higher and further education, the police and the voluntary sector. Others again (and in particular those at regional and sub-regional level) have board or management membership appointed by central government. Many boxes in Figure 7.1, and especially those at city and neighbourhood level, take the form of an open and inclusive partnership whose formal membership may be unknown to many participant organisations, where observers turn up to speak and indeed participate in decision taking. Relationships are in some cases hierarchical, in some cases informal, with chains of command and control reaching in some cases directly downwards from central government to the smallest area level, but in other cases moving through a hierarchy of levels with intervening organisations exercising delegated (and, to varying degrees, discretionary) responsibility.

The overall thrust of the government's proposals for local government are less towards the recreation of local democracy and more towards modernisation, most obviously captured by the requirement for the restructuring of local authorities along the executive and scrutiny model. The executive cabinet model (or elected mayor model were that to spread to Bristol) allows leading members to negotiate and take decisions on key matters and to some extent frees them to be more proactive in inter-organisational bargaining and collaborative decision making. In the executive cabinet model it is less obvious that matters

discussed in a partnership need to be taken back for approval by committee or council. The criticism that the public sector cannot bring weight and commitment to the partnership table becomes less valid, and in principle joint decision making is easier. Accountability on the other hand becomes blurred. To whom do the various partnership structures report? What is the relationship between accountability to partnership and accountability to partner organisations? How does the scrutiny function work in relation to inter-organisational working?

Yet discussion of democracy in general, and representative democracy in particular, must recognise the centrality of political survival and control on collaboration and conflict in the city-region. Differing party political control in South Gloucestershire and Bristol, the vulnerability of a Labour-run city council to Liberal Democrat political gains, together with the sensitivity of housing land release and permissions as a local political issue, combined to create an environment within which collaboration was at best hard work, and at worst an ongoing dog fight. This was never more obvious than in the strategic sub-regional planning arena where the legacy of an inadequate local government reorganisation which failed to create the capacity for strategic planning lives on (see Chapter 3 of this volume).

An urban regime?

Bristol has been the subject of community power studies for over half a century (Miller, 1958a, 1958b; Clements, 1969). Transfer of regime theory to Europe is difficult, given the complex relationship of central to local state as well as the fact that the roots of regime theory remain in the growth machine tradition in the US (Logan and Molotch, 1987; Harding, 1994; Stoker and Mossberger, 1994; Lauria, 1997). Nevertheless it has been possible to identify the emergence of coalitions and alliances which begin to resemble the regimes of the US literature (Owen, 1994; Peck and Tickell, 1995; Valler, 1995; Haughton and Williams, 1996).

A regime reflects the capacity of local leadership (combining private and public sectors) to develop a strategic vision and coordinate both their own and other stakeholders' actions. Stone (1989) argues that a "regime is specifically about the *informal arrangements* that surround and complement the formal workings of governmental authority" (emphasis in original). Sustainable regimes rely on interpersonal relations and the development of trust, predictability and reliability. They work across institutional/organisational boundaries and require a capacity for what Stone terms 'understanding' or 'social learning' whereby the partners in a coalition engage in a process of 'mutual account taking'. Social learning may have the effect of intensifying collaboration, redefining the identity of the individual partners, and thereby producing a more inclusive and cohesive identify for the regime.

In Bristol, DiGaetano and Klemanski (2000) concluded that Bristol represents a very wide governing coalition encompassing a traditional (in regime terms) pro-growth agenda but also a growth management agenda. Although their perception was that there is "a prevailing coalition which may be transforming into a regime", the evidence from their long-term view reinforces other work which suggests a very fragile coalition/regime if such indeed exists (Bassett, 1993). Stewart (1996) identified an 'incipient regime'. Certainly the competitive and loosely organised network relationships which until recently characterised the city-region scarcely resemble the coalitions and regimes which are identified in the North American literature on cities and power.

This stems in part from the absence of clear focus for collaborative action. The private sector is motivated by a competitive growth agenda, albeit tempered by deep concerns about social cohesion. This is reflected in the growing attention being given by the private sector to the sub-regional agenda in an attempt to shape the region's development strategy and place Bristol and the West of England at the heart of the region's economic strategy. Much energy has thus been expended on the West of England Strategic Partnership (WESP), the machinery through which SWERDA reaches down to the constituent parts of the region. Indeed, until government defined the local authority area as the norm for LSPs, the Chamber of Commerce saw WESP as the obvious LSP for the city-region. Bristol sat uneasily within WESP, and the relative role of WESP and the emergent Bristol LSP has remained to be fully worked through. This was a reflection of the fragile

post-local government reorganisation linkages between four strong unitary authorities and the historically uneasy relationship between Bristol and its hinterland. There was much joint working and joint action between partners but less sense of cohesion or strategy, and Bristol's *urban* focus has been weakly articulated in both sub-regional and regional forums. In practice, four of the first board members of SWERDA came from Bristol; other city activists were present on a variety of regional groups; and there was extensive networking across the region. Notwithstanding this membership of, and active participation in, regional structures, urban interests remained weakly articulated in a region where the rural voice is a strong one.

Within the city, a range of stakeholders are present in most of the city-wide and neighbourhood partnership arrangements. The organised voluntary sector, working through VOSCUR (Voluntary Organisations Standing Conference on Urban Regeneration), plays an important role in city-wide and sub-city structures and in so doing enhances the non-statutory voice in the networks of regeneration, although at the same time is felt to exclude direct community representation on the new institutional map. There has, for example, been no direct community grass-roots representation at any level in the SRB structures, with established voluntary sector actors arguing that the place for direct community representation is at the level of projects (Purdue et al, 2000). Indeed, the role of umbrella voluntary organisations in the mediation of regeneration activity between council and community has long been a source of tension, a tension accentuated by the absence of a Council for Voluntary Service in the city and a consequent competition among some other players for the position, status and resources which occupying such a position might bring.

Network governance and collaborative capacity

Network governance

The distinction between three paradigms of governance – market, hierarchy and network – has already been made. There is clear evidence in Bristol of the coexistence of these paradigms. It took a decade for the failure of two City Challenge bids to convince a grudging city council that it was necessary to compete against other localities for resources from Whitehall and Brussels. City Challenge, SRB funding, Objective 2 designation and the Lottery Funds all had in different ways alerted the city to the need to win resources against domestic and international competition. At the time of writing, the City of Culture 2008 bid was taking up the time and energy of a wide range of local stakeholders. The market mode is now well entrenched. Equally, the presence of hierarchy is clearly visible. The institutional map recognises the continuing downwards pressure from central government on localities. The implementation style of much of the local government modernisation debate, of the many ABIs, and of European programmes remains in many respects top-down, bureaucratic and hierarchical. The experience of Bristol's Community at Heart NDC scheme certainly exemplifies a real change in the relationship between local stakeholders, and has offered some shift towards participative democracy at the expense of the traditional structures of power. It has been accompanied, however, locally and nationally, by a burden of bureaucratic procedure that has done much to exhaust and burn out both community and statutory sector actors. Most recently, the requirement for LSPs reflects the pressure from the centre on localities, and while offering some local autonomy reinforces the hierarchical nature of British public administration.

The important continuing coexistence of market and hierarchy modes must be acknowledged, therefore; but the most obvious aspect of the new urban governance remains its network characteristics. Network theory has been a favoured perspective over the past decade, but the network model has been widely criticised as being merely descriptive and lacking in a perspective on power. Different perspectives on the structures of influence and power at work in Bristol – theories of democracy, of the state and central–local relations, and of coalitions and regimes as discussed earlier in this chapter – invite questions about the drivers of inter-organisational collaboration and about the extent to which network governance is sufficient to build the collaborative capacity needed to fulfil the requirements of local strategic partnership working.

It is clear that, in the South West in general and Bristol in particular, there is extensive networking, as individuals assemble and reassemble in successive partnership or initiative meetings. The cross-partnership interlocking nature of the leadership structures in the city-region is clear. 'Cliques in concert' was felt to be an appropriate label to describe community power structures in Bristol almost 50 years ago (Miller, 1958a), and, give or take a few discordant notes, this label still appears applicable, even if the cliques are more open than before.

These tendencies had been evident for decades. A study of community power in Bristol in the late 1950s (Miller, 1958a, 1958b) identified a mixture of elected civic leaders and business interests who appeared to run Bristol. The picture was of

... a pattern of influence best described as a kaleidoscope of recognisable faces shifting in and out of fluid coalitions as issues change.

If 'coalitional fluidity' is one characteristic of the network, collaborative inertia (Huxham and Vangen, 2000) may be another. Certainly on paper there is evidence of the potential for a highly developed and effective collaborative capacity networked across all sectors, and indeed Bristol illustrates the institutional thickness discussed by Thrift and Amin. This might be, however, as indicative of a congested institutional space as of a rich and interactive one. A culture of partnership working has been established and consolidated over the past decade (and even perhaps a shadowy regime evolved). In the run up to the formation of a LSP in the city, however, the evidence was that while a strong network might be a necessary condition of successful long-term collaborative capacity it is not in itself sufficient.

This may in part be because the power relationships inherent in both the vertical and horizontal arrangements tend to be under-recognised. This is most obviously the case where new political arrangements are being constructed at the regional level (regional assembly, RDA, government office, inter alia) and at the city level (with executive and scrutiny bringing new roles for council and councillors). It is more so in the more opaque fields of governance where inter-organisational network linkages based on trust and reciprocity combine with more formalised relationships of government. The discussion of central–local relations, of democracy, and regimes in the previous part of this chapter only hints at the complex power struggles which characterise Bristol and, of course, any other city. The characteristic of the new network governance is the capacity to manage the power differentials between stakeholders and to negotiate, broker, arrange, or construct action that creates collaborative advantage shared by all parties. Collaborative capacity is the ability to generate this advantage through joint decision and action within at least partly voluntary arrangements. The setting up of LSPs represents the culmination in the government's attempts to generate such local capacity and it is Bristol's moves towards the establishment of an LSP which illustrate the challenges faced by all localities in translating the network governance of partnership into a more formalised LSP.

Local Strategic Partnerships

The concept of the LSP was central to the Urban Policy White Paper and to the implementation of policies for both competition and cohesion. Twin-tracked through the guidance for Community Planning on the one hand (DETR, 2000e) and for Neighbourhood Renewal on the other hand (SEU, 2001), LSPs are seen as the vehicle through which main programmes can address local community objectives in general and social inclusion objectives in particular. Local Strategic Partnerships are expected to fulfil a number of tasks: preparation of a Community Strategy, rationalisation of local partnerships and contribution to floor targets. Their formal accreditation was in large part built on a self-assessment process, but the final recommendation to ministers on accreditation came from the government office.

Bristol is one of the 88 localities that required an LSP in order to access Neighbourhood Renewal Funds for the year 2002/03. In its developmental stages, the Bristol LSP struggled to establish the conditions under which the partnership could become effective and receive accreditation (DTLR, 2001b). At the outset, a 70-member Council (unfortunately so named given the need for the LSP to be clearly non-city council dominated) was supported by a 24-member Executive Programme Delivery Group as well as by a number of Theme Groups which

would draw together a number of pre-existing areas of partnership working – Lifelong Learning, Economy, Health and Well-Being, Environment, and Local Communities. A Neighbourhood Strategy involved the development of a number of Neighbourhood Partnerships across the city which would be represented on, and feed into, the Theme Groups and the LSP itself.

From the outset, the Bristol LSP was relatively unusual. Its 'core group' (the executive delivery group with a memberships of 24) was larger than the full LSP of many other areas, and the 70-strong full membership, while providing a broad and inclusive forum for debate about community issues, might have lacked the capacity to generate strategic decisions. The delivery group might well be able to formulate the required action plan but there were early concerns about the capacity of the LSP to push forward action (at least action that would not have taken place in any case), about the extent of community and voluntary sector engagement, and about the culture of partnership working. Soon, however, the real politics of accreditation began to dominate. An inner-core group (the 'secret six') met to start the formulation of a strategy which would warrant GOSW endorsement, retain the engagement of the six major spending players, yet preserve the involvement of the wider group of statutory and community stakeholders. In effect, the initial structure was inverted with the pyramid of influence and power coming to a narrow rather than wide peak. In 2002, the reality of the tension between inclusion and effectiveness has been reflected in proposals that the membership of the LSP be reduced to some two dozen in total, and that other routes towards access and inclusion be sought – through neighbourhood structures and through participation in thematic working groups.

Whether the Bristol LSP should or should not have been accredited at a particular point in time is not an issue for this book. What is more important is to consider the broader lessons for the building of collaborative capacity which derive from the experience of a city where there is a long history both of complacency and conflict as well as a more recent history of positive partnership working. The Bristol LSP encapsulates, often in an exaggerated form, many of the problems which have been identified as confronting LSPs generally, but which are not explicitly acknowledged as problematic in the governmental guidance.

Dilemmas in the new urban governance

The new urban governance as currently practised involves all three governmental paradigms of market, hierarchy and network. There remains a competitive element requiring competition between localities for resources, the regeneration process remains in many ways bureaucratic and multi-sector networking is encouraged. It has been argued (Stewart, 2002) that this involves an excess and confusion of governmental style. Urban change should be predominantly through either market, hierarchy, or network modes, but not through all at the same time.

However, while, in general, urban governance appears to involve too many modes, whichever mode applies in any city – and it may be that different modes may be appropriate in different places – it is important that there are robust structures and practices to support it. As argued earlier, Bristol has responded partially to all three modes. The need to compete for resources, to manage the bureaucracy of urban initiatives, and to develop some form of networked governance is evident in the city, but the evidence suggests that all three modes are relatively weak. It is certainly the case that there has been institutional proliferation and this chapter has illustrated the complexity of the vertical and horizontal structures that characterise sub-national governance. This is an excess of the institutional thickness which Amin and Thrift (1995) identified as the key features of the new governance. Indeed the appropriate diagnosis might be a weakening through sclerosis rather than strengthening. Despite this institutional proliferation, however, or perhaps because of it, the Bristol city-region appears to have experienced a lack of governmental capacity in general and collaborative network capacity in particular. The evidence has been of a weakly integrated system of multi-level, multi-sector arrangements, characterised by the absence of appropriate inter-organisational arrangements and inter-partnership protocols. The Bristol city-region appears less effective than it might because it has lacked both the administrative-cum-bureaucratic certainty which a system of hierarchy,

and the confidence and trust which a strong network system, might bring.

This is not untypical at a time when network and hierarchy governance are being combined through arrangements such as LSPs; but Bristol provides some explanation of why some cities experience more difficulty in conforming to the requirements of network governance than others. Three factors stand out from the analysis – historical and contemporary – of Bristol, the West of England, and the South West region.

1. *Civic identity* is central to effective working in urban partnership. Multi-level governance places heavy demands on all players, as a neighbourhood-cum-community paradigm requires greater recognition of and responsiveness to very localised issues, while a rejuvenated regionalism demands active engagement with governance above the city level. The Janus analogy – looking two ways at once (Stewart, 1998, 2000) – remains appropriate for a city that seems unable to manage the tasks of relating simultaneously outwards to the region and inwards to the local community. On the one hand, there is a more outward-looking style than hitherto. Bristol is active in European networks and is involved in a wide range of joint working in sub-regional partnership at several levels. Leading members participate in the regional debate. Jokes about CUBA (County that Used to Be Avon) reflect recognition that, functionally if not politically, the city-region has a coherence that demands a unified approach to some issues, especially in the face of competition from other sub-regions. Nevertheless, the city guards its independence and autonomy carefully to the extent that this is seen by others as isolated and introspective. There has been a consequent loss of capacity to influence the external debate and a weakening in the collaborative capacity of the city-region as a whole. A former council leader maintained a low profile in external affairs and the former chief executive, a key player in the new governance in recent years, left Bristol, rumoured to have been too visible in external networks at the expense of the political leadership. The city council has thus been present in many sub-regional and regional fora but its role has been neither explicit nor accountable. There was thus a weak civic identity, a weakness perhaps

accentuated by more than 20 years of two-tier government in which the city council lost power and status.

2. The research evidence suggests a widespread perception that *leadership* – organisational and individual – has been weak within the city-region. Parallel research within the ESRC Cities programme identified Bristol as illustrating a situation of loose governance where multi-organisational partnerships co-exist in a fragmented system, and where no single organisation or person offers clear direction. Instead, a number of potential leaders hold multiple membership of several partnerships which may imply the presence of integrated leadership but in practice may fail to offer it. Thus leadership is 'implied and fragmented', operating without strategic direction. It has been recognised that the arrangements for partnership working move through successive phases as their role and functions evolve over time (Snape and Stewart, 1995; Skelcher and Lowndes, 1998). The shifting pattern of partnership working in the Bristol city-region emphasises this point as new regional, sub-regional and neighbourhood partnerships supplement the more long-standing city partnership arrangements. What is evident throughout, however, is both the pervasive bureaucratic style of partnership working and the demands which simply operating the system impose on leaders, and the demands which network management make on those who frequent many collaborative settings. The effect may be to enhance transactional and contingent leadership, diminishing the potential of visionary or charismatic leadership. What seems clear in Bristol, as elsewhere, is that for the new LSP to work effectively in the interests of citizens, a more visible and proactive leadership will be needed both to manage the rationalisation which LSPs call for and sustain the spirit and philosophy of partnership working. There is evidence indeed that such a leadership is now emerging.

3. The notion of *social capital* involves not only a concern with local social interaction, weak and strong ties, and mutuality at local community or neighbourhood level but also a concern with the relationship between state and civil society (Woolcock, 1998; Taylor, 2000; Stewart, 2002). This raises questions about the relationship between state and civil society in general and

about the connections between the organisations of governance and community in particular. This is, in part, a function of the relative strengths of the democratic systems at work in a city, and we have argued that there is in Bristol a tension between representative and participative democracy. It is also in part a function of the levels of trust between different sectors and the extent to which there is recognised mutual interest between (and indeed within) public, private, voluntary and community sectors. Despite a number of arenas for inter-sectoral exchange and learning – not least a strong Common Purpose – Bristol's stock of social capital often appears low, with a lingering legacy of suspicion and mistrust (Miller, 1999). The challenge of addressing new governance appears less to encourage new forms of interdependent collaboration, and more to press key actors into defensive positions protective of their particular interests. The city council in particular was been slow to engage with the new agenda. The style of governance appears to have been one of risk minimisation and management rather than positive forward governance within a shared civic agenda.

In conclusion, the strategic capacity of Bristol is latent rather than evident. There has been extensive development of partnership working, with the private sector taking the lead in many joint initiatives. However, in a complex and volatile institutional setting, and with central government introducing repeated innovations in local experimentation, there has been little coherence to strategic capacity building. This is the product of a weakness in all three of the factors identified in this chapter: civic identity, leadership and social capital.

Taken together, the absence of these three elements in combination appears to weaken the adaptive capacity of the city-region. While there is no unambiguous definition of adaptive capacity, it involves the capacity to change direction, to respond to a shifting environment, to mobilise and deploy resources flexibly to meet new circumstances and to work collaboratively in coalitions. The emergence of LSPs aims to capture a number of attributes of collaborative working. They should be strategic, inclusive, action focused, performance managed, efficient and provide for learning and development. The experience of Bristol, however, demonstrates the difficulties of generating such attributes in a short period of time. The Bristol analysis shows how the weight of past practice influences attitudes and behaviour. It is difficult to shake off a historic conservatism, to shift from risk minimisation to risk taking, to establish a trusting and robust culture of partnership and to extract collaborative advantage. Like a good orchestra, civic partnerships need extensive rehearsal and strong strategic partnerships resemble an orchestra – a shared score, efficient instruments and skilled players in harmony under a good conductor.

Genuine adaptive strategic capacity requires months, even years, of practice, years of inter-organisational learning and years of building trust. Bristol has not practised this form of behaviour consistently over past years, and will require a number of years to learn. The generalised lesson is that effective partnership working and the development of collaborative capacity cannot simply be externally imposed; rather, it will vary with the local context, with the perceived policy challenges and the historic legacy of local political structures and culture.

8

Conclusions: shaping the urban future

Martin Boddy

This final chapter brings together key findings from the Bristol study and draws out lessons and implications of broader relevance. It focuses in turn on issues of competitive advantage, the broad impacts of policy and governance, links between competitiveness and social cohesion and the implications of urban renaissance. It then looks at the implications of new forms of 'multi-nodal' urban development and the impacts of administrative fragmentation. It concludes by considering lessons for the effective management of urban growth in the context of the government's new commitment to 'sustainable communities', pointing to the crucial importance of the new spatial architecture of governance to the future shaping of urban development across the country as a whole.

The roots of competitive advantage

Considerable effort has been expended, not least in the context of the ESRC Cities Programme, in attempting to determine the bases of urban competitive advantage – what helps particular urban areas to succeed where others struggle (Begg, 2002). Different accounts of competitive advantage have stressed the role of different forms of clustering as the basis for agglomeration economies and scale effects (including labour market pooling, specialist inputs and services, and knowledge and information flows) and the key role of un-traded interdependencies (trust, cooperation and the transfer of tacit knowledge). Other approaches stress the role of particular lead sectors as economic drivers of an emergent knowledge economy and more specifically innovation and entrepreneurship. Begg (1999) distinguishes the influences on urban performance of

sectoral trends, including the inherited mix of activities; company characteristics; the business environment including various factors of production, social and environmental factors and the variety of agglomeration effects; and capacity for innovation and learning. A variation on this, using an assets model which draws on indicators relating to economic, policy, environmental and social contexts, places Bristol fourth among English urban areas in terms of its asset base (Deas and Giordano, 2002).

The findings from the Bristol case study in fact emphasise the importance of a relatively conventional set of factors in underpinning the sub-region's long-term economic buoyancy. These include proximity to London; good motorway and rail communications; relatively good access to international air travel; and a ready supply of land and property with different characteristics, including the choice between central area and urban fringe locations. These are at one level relatively unremarkable and do not draw upon anything very technically sophisticated in the form of analysis. They are, on the other hand, very solidly supported by the evidence including business surveys and detailed information-gathering from employers and other organisations in the sub-region and beyond. Quality of life, the attractiveness and profile of the city and surrounding rural areas, cultural and leisure provision and the consequent ability of the sub-region to attract and retain a wide range of professional, technical and other labour have also been an important component of the overall assets of the sub-region. This has facilitated both the attraction of inwards investment and also indigenous expansion. It has also sustained and expanded the 'knowledge base' of the sub-regional economy – this is particularly significant given the widely acknowledged importance of 'the knowledge economy' broadly defined, as the basis for competitive success.

Different approaches have argued the importance of industrial clusters, of innovation or of particular 'key sectors' in driving competitive success. As indicated in Chapters 4 and 5, there is some evidence for the existence of industrial clusters in the sense developed in recent analyses in both financial services and in the culture and media sectors. However, these are limited in scale and in terms of their overall impact even within these two sectors. There is no real evidence from the case study more generally, including business surveys, that clusters and the processes of positive feedback or agglomeration associated with such clusters, plays any particular role in driving the sub-regional economy. One 'city-size' or agglomeration effect which does appear to be important is the scale and variety of the sub-regional labour market and skill pool – economic theory argues that both workers and businesses benefit from locating in such a labour market pool which offers flexibility and scope to both parties. This ties back to the importance of the knowledge base and the knowledge economy.

Other studies have stressed the association between innovation and more competitive localities – in the case of England, the concentration of innovation in London and the south east (Simmie, 2002). National objectives with regard to competitiveness and growth have also driven concern with innovation and the role of research and development. It is not clear, however, that innovation as such is driving wealth creation or competitive success in particular localities in any very direct way. It may well be the case, rather, that the more competitive localities and those which can attract highly skilled professional and technical labour tend to be those that also generate the sorts of innovative activity captured in such analyses. The case of Bristol provides no evidence of any particular role for innovation and innovative activity in terms of overall economic performance. Nor does the Bristol case support the role of particular sectors as the key drivers of economic success – high technology and aerospace, financial services and the knowledge-based activities in the cultural and media sectors have been and remain important components of the sub-regional economy. It is, however, the combination of these (and other

sectors) that accounts for the overall competitive strength of the sub-region. If anything, it has been the ability of the sub-region to attract and support a wide range of different economic sectors that has accounted for its relative success in economic terms. Diverse types of economic activity have shared a common attraction to the particular bundle of assets offered by the city-region.

Policy and governance

The lessons and implications for policy and governance in the sense of creating or reproducing competitive advantage are, if anything, quite limited. Factors such as quality of life and 'liveability' are to a large extent a product of location and long historical process. They do, however, point to the importance in policy terms of maintaining and enhancing whatever assets exist in any particular locality. They also emphasise the particular and increasing importance of such factors in the context of the knowledge economy. They perhaps also point to the need to cater in particular for the needs and tastes of professional and technical groups in the labour market in terms of housing, cultural and leisure provision and environment – pointing in a sense to a somewhat elitist vision of urban renaissance, should competitiveness be the key aim. In this sense, cultural policy and cultural investment have a double significance, as both economic sectors of growing importance in their own right, but also as contributing to the overall image and attractiveness of particular localities to key labour market groups and business investment.

Bristol's experience also points to the particular role of planning and land availability in relation to competitive success. As detailed in Chapter 3, the permissive planning regime established in the 1970s on Bristol's north fringe was crucial to the subsequent rapid expansion of investment and development. It was not, as explained earlier, part of any overall strategic framework for the development of the city-region as a whole. The nature and quality of the development that resulted were problematic in a number of respects, as detailed earlier. But as the Bristol case study shows, it amounted in effect to a de facto growth strategy for the next 25 years or more, which has been crucial to the competitive strength of the city-region as a whole. The study also suggests the potential damaging effects of policy aiming to restrict further growth on the city's north fringe. In policy terms, this points to the potentially key role of the planning system in shaping and enabling economic expansion in the context of relatively high demand areas in southern England. It also points to the need for proactive growth management in order to secure high quality, sustainable development that underpins the competitive strength of the economy at regional and national scales. And it points to the potential dangers of unduly restricting development in locations that business investors see as providing the basis for competitive success.

Competitiveness and social exclusion

As described in Chapter 2, Bristol represents a large and relatively prosperous southern city that has performed well in economic terms against regional and national benchmarks. Despite this, as detailed in Chapter 3, the city-region includes marked spatial concentrations of unemployment, poverty and deprivation. Several wards are among the worst in the country in terms of the government's composite index of deprivation – five wards, including both inner-city areas and outer estates, are in the worst 10% of wards in England. The worst, Lawrence Hill in the core inner city was worst, ranked 133rd out of 8,414 wards nationally. Extremes of deprivation are moreover juxtaposed with neighbourhoods with particularly low levels of deprivation in a pattern of quite marked spatial polarisation across the city as a whole. Educational deprivation is also particularly marked in Bristol city itself, with Filwood ward, covering part of south Bristol's outer estates, ranked 7th from bottom nationally out of 8,414 and three adjoining wards were in the worst 100 nationally. This represents a remarkable degree of deprivation for a city such as Bristol. It is reflected as well in school performance statistics and this is particularly significant given the critical role of educational attainment in determining social exclusion and deprivation later in life, as explained in Chapter 6.

The case of Bristol very clearly demonstrates that competitive success and relative economic buoyancy in overall terms by no means eliminates the sort of spatially concentrated deprivation and polarisation

associated with cities much worse off in economic terms. Many in the local population clearly do benefit from the city's overall success, and the overall level of demand in the labour market compared with cities such as Liverpool or Glasgow is clearly beneficial. But what is equally clear, is that significant sections of the local population benefit little from the opportunities that are generated. The Bristol case makes it clear that competitive success is not in itself sufficient to combat significant levels of spatially concentrated deprivation. It suggests that patterns of occupational and labour market change have led to considerable polarisation with a concentration of low-paid often temporary or insecure jobs.

Beyond this, however, it demonstrates the impacts of a wider set of processes of social exclusion, including educational deprivation, on sections of the population who are disconnected or only loosely connected to the formal labour market. In broad policy terms this emphasises the need to address social exclusion and its impacts independently of measures to address competitiveness – given that increased competitive strength is not necessarily reflected in lower levels of social exclusion and social deprivation. Social exclusion needs to be addressed in its own right as a major issue of social justice and equality. Evidence also points to the importance of measures aimed at combating social exclusion that extend beyond the package of 'welfare-to-work' programmes which aim to reconnect different groups to the labour market. It also re-emphasises the central importance of addressing educational engagement and attainment and pre-school activities – as recognised by a range of recent policy measures.

The research programme as a whole also addressed the related question of the extent to which the competitiveness of urban areas might be undermined by social exclusion and its symptoms in terms of spatially concentrated unemployment and deprivation. The Bristol study in fact found no evidence that marked levels of deprivation in parts of the city-region adversely affected neither business location nor investment. Lack of investment in south Bristol, for example, was reported to reflect poor accessibility and lack of suitable sites compared with the north fringe or central Bristol, rather than concern over levels of social exclusion and deprivation. Nor was the marked under-performance of pupils in the state education sector in

Bristol seen as a particular issue from the perspective of competitiveness. Businesses tended instead to cite the quality of the private sector in the city of Bristol and of state schools in the surrounding districts as a positive asset. This reinforces findings from other city case studies including Liverpool and Glasgow. They also found little evidence for any adverse impacts on competitiveness generated by social exclusion – the 'business case' for addressing social exclusion is in this sense unsupported although it can be argued that high levels of social exclusion represent a wasted or under-utilised asset in a wider sense. Again, however, the imperative to address social exclusion is essentially based on social justice.

Urban renaissance

Bristol clearly demonstrates the capacity of urban areas outside of London to achieve elements of urban renaissance along the lines advocated by the Urban Task Force and promoted, subsequently, by the White Paper, the Urban Summit and a range of government initiatives. The 2001 Population Census may have dashed hoped-for headlines of population growth in the urban core. Employment growth remains strong, however, and expanding household numbers have buoyed housing demand. Government policy and exhortation to focus development on brownfield sites can also take credit for directing developer attention to new house building and conversion in city-centre locations. There has been a resurgence of new high-density housing including high-profile harbourside developments, together with office development and leisure provision that has transformed parts of the core urban area. This is very much in line with the overall thrust of government thinking in the post-Task Force era.

In practical terms, however, it also poses questions for the government's model of urban renaissance – labelled by some as "state-sponsored gentrification" (Lees, 2000, p 391). This, as argued elsewhere (Lambert and Boddy, 2002), is something of a misnomer. The processes at work are rather different from earlier phases of colonisation of older housing by middle-class households and the displacement of lower-income residents. The thrust of the criticism in terms of social impacts and implications is, however, borne out by the Bristol experience. Much of the residential development has been targeted on

relatively well-off single people or households. There has been little provision of social and community facilities including public sector provision that would support more in the way of families and a broader social and demographic mix. The volume of affordable housing that has been secured on the back of these developments has also, as yet, been very limited. Renaissance is largely reflected, therefore, in what is a relatively exclusive form of development and repopulation of the city. This clearly raises serious questions that need to be confronted more generally in the push for urban renaissance. Government has recognised and started to address the particular issue of housing affordability (ODPM, 2003c). The difficulty of securing such provision in the case of Bristol, on the back of apparently profitable, upmarket developments and in a relatively buoyant housing market suggests, however, that this will be difficult to achieve in practice.

The polycentric city-region

Renewed investment in Bristol's core urban area, including large-scale commercial and mixed use development, has been seen locally as reinforcing the centrality of the traditional city-centre focus for economic activity. This was something of a relief for those who feared that edge-city development threatened to suck the life out of the traditional urban core, the denuding of downtown seen as typical of many US cities. This has clearly not happened and the resurgence of investment and activity at the core of the city-region is clearly to be welcomed. At the same time, as described in the preceding chapters of this report, the city's north fringe has developed as a significant focus for investment and development in its own right and a major contributor to the competitiveness of the city-region as a whole. It offered a different set of characteristics to the city centre. Growth rates in terms of employment and population remain well above those for the city-region as a whole. It also continues to offer major potential for the future in terms of attracting investment and economic activity and in ensuring the continuing competitiveness of the city-region as a whole.

This polycentric pattern of urban development is typical of many urban areas across the UK, whether through edge-city types of development as with

Bristol or Edinburgh for example (Bramley and Lambert, 2002) or through linked networks or urban nodes in a more extended sub-regional context (Cooke et al, 2002). What is important is that the policy context and the planning framework in particular, along with infrastructure provision, administrative and political structures relate to these developments. It is vital that these both recognise and respond in a positive and proactive way to these shifts in urban form. Urban renaissance, densification and investment in the urban core are key aims. Central urban areas retain a vital economic role, which has been reinforced by recent patterns of investment. However, this should not lead to policies based on the misguided assumption that we can recreate the traditional, monocentric cities where everything revolves around the Central Business District or downtown. Ensuring the full contribution of cities to competitiveness at regional and national levels requires that policy and planning frameworks respond to the structure and dynamics of complex urban systems.

Administrative fragmentation

The implications of administrative and political fragmentation, split between the four local authorities responsible for parts of the Bristol city-region as a whole have been noted earlier. This problem is by no means unique to this sub-region. However, here, as elsewhere, it reflects earlier incomplete and politically over-determined attempts at local government reform. In less economically buoyant parts of the country, however, there would seem to be a greater willingness to transcend fragmentation and to pursue common goals at least at the level of economic strategy and infrastructure provision. In the case of Bristol, the economic imperative has been less pressing and the need to collaborate (and the penalties of failing to do so), therefore, less immediately apparent.

Bristol city-region has clearly performed well in economic terms relative to many other urban areas in Britain as a whole. Arguably, however, with a greater degree of strategic direction and collective vision it could have done considerably better in terms of economic outcomes, infrastructure and service provision, sustainability and quality of life. Laissez-faire planning in the 1970s and 1980s provided the

basis for the development boom on the north fringe. It did little, however, to ensure the effective management of that growth, the quality of the overall development or its integration within the city-region as a whole. Failure to secure any form of effective public transport infrastructure was also (and remains) a conspicuous failure. In part, this reflects a lack of coordination and, at times, conflict in terms of political direction and policy intent between the constituent local councils. In part, it also reflects the sort of localism promoted by relatively small administrative areas and the short-term goals of party political control and which is perhaps an inevitable outcome of this sort of fragmentation.

What has clearly been lacking is any form of strategic vision at the level of the functional city-region as a whole, let alone the will to pursue such a vision in practice. The Bristol-city region is perhaps an extreme example of this. However, it is an issue, more generally, over other parts of the country as a whole. This lack of fit between existing administrative and political structures and clear need for city-region-scale vision and strategy remain a major obstacle to many of the government's objectives in terms of urban policy and spatial strategy. They also threaten to undermine the economic performance and contribution of the country's major urban areas. A further round of local government reorganisation would be the rational solution. The aim would be to ensure that the boundaries of primary administrative and political units coincide with – or ideally extend slightly beyond – the extent of functional urban areas. Local government reform of this nature is likely, however, to be highly unpopular at a local level and has certainly not been seen as a priority by central government.

An alternative scenario is that the new regional agenda might provide more of a strategic focus at the sub-regional or city-region scale. In the case of the South West, Regional Planning Guidance has, as yet, done little to challenge the status quo. It refers to the administrative area of Bristol City as a 'principal urban area' in its own right, along with Bath and Weston-super-Mare which are seen as separate entities rather than part of a wider sub-regional whole. The development of Regional Spatial Strategies for each of the regions, together with the fundamental changes envisaged in the statutory planning framework does, however, provide a potential opportunity to establish the strategic role of the sub-regional level. This could, for example, provide the opportunity to reinforce the role of the 'core cities', Bristol included, as coherent city-regions with a clear strategic focus on securing competitiveness and quality of life. The danger is that strategy is dragged down once again by local concerns and short-term political expediencies.

The management of urban growth

The lessons provided by Bristol's experience of urban expansion and the lack of strategic policy context for the effective management of urban growth in the sub-region have particular relevance for the implementation of the government's current 'communities plan' set out in *Creating sustainable communities: Building for the future* (ODPM, 2003a). Following on from the Urban Task Force, the White Paper and revised Planning Policy Guidance (ODPM, 2003b), major emphasis has been placed on the channelling of new housing development onto previously developed brownfield sites within existing urban areas. Questions can be raised as to how effectively this has been achieved in practice and in particular the social impacts and implications as noted earlier. In general terms, however, it has very rightly been at the core of the government's urban strategy.

What has been missing, however, has been provision for the effective, proactive planning and management of new settlement on greenfield sites on or beyond the urban fringe. This is vital, given the scale of new housing development needed to accommodate the projected major growth in household numbers. However successful the strategy of brownfield development, a major part of this growth in households will inevitably have to be met by new greenfield settlements. Bristol's experience points to the consequences of relatively unplanned responses to growth pressures. Locally, moreover, in Bristol as elsewhere, there remains resistance to further housing development on anything like the scale needed to accommodate demographic and economic pressures.

Creating sustainable communities goes some way to address these issues. It outlines plans for delivering new and expanded settlements based on principles to achieve broadly defined 'sustainable communities'.

Much of the impetus behind this 'action plan' clearly came from the perceived need to "accommodate the economic success of London and the wider South East and ensure that the international competitiveness of the region is sustained for the benefit of the region and the whole country" (ODPM, 2003a, p 46). It identified four main growth areas within the South East including Thames Gateway, Milton Keynes/South Midland, Ashford and London-Stansted-Cambridge. There were separate 'action plans' covering each of the other regions, including the South West, but much of the government's emphasis, and the detailed development of proposals since the original action plan, has focused on London and the South East (ODPM, 2003a).

There has been much less attention on how to accommodate pressures for growth and housing development beyond London and the South East. Bristol, in the context of the South West region, is a particular case in point given the scale of projected household growth and the additional pressures generated by the competitive success of the city-region and the region as a whole. However, it is a wider issue, particularly given the government's aim of securing the competitiveness of the wider set of core cities and their contribution to regional and national prosperity. The so-called regional 'action plans' were in any case more statements of intent than any form of detailed plans for actions and implementation. Serious attention is needed to develop appropriate strategic frameworks and delivery mechanisms for new and expanded sustainable communities beyond London and the South East. Government has provided very little in the way of new provisions or guidance as to what form these might take. Again, the onus is being placed on 'the regional partners' – the government's regional offices, regional assemblies, RDAs and English Partnerships in particular – to implement, or in effect develop and flesh out these 'action plans'. How effectively this can be achieved in practice remains to be seen. Suffice to say that it is placing a heavy load on the main regional partners and other institutional partners at regional and sub-regional scales. It would also require the regional partners to prioritise and promote expanded or new settlements in a very proactive way. This might be difficult to achieve given the imperative placed on regional institutions, to balance the needs of different communities across the whole of their regional territories. What is clear is that the development of this new spatial architecture of governance and the extent to which it is able to provide for vision and strategic direction at a sub-regional level will be critical in terms of shaping the future of the country's major urban areas, Bristol included.

References

Adburgham, R. (1998) *Bristol: Partnership in governance – 10 years of The Bristol Initiative*, Bristol: The Redcliffe Press.

Allmendinger, P. and Thomas, H. (eds) (1998) *Urban planning and the British new right*, London: Routledge.

Amin, A. and Thrift, N. (1995a) 'Institutional issues for the European regions: from markets and plans to socioeconomics and powers of association', *Economy and Society*, vol 24, no 1, pp 41-66.

Amin, A. and Thrift, N. (1995b) 'Globalisation, institutional thickness and the local economy', in P. Healey, S. Cameron, S. Davoudi, S. Graham, and A. Madin-Pour (eds) Chichester: John Wiley, pp 91-108.

Atkinson, A. (1998) 'Social exclusion, poverty and unemployment', in A. Atkinson and J. Hills (eds) *Exclusion, employment and opportunity*, Centre for the Analysis of Social Exclusion Paper 4, London: London School of Economics and Political Science, pp 1-20.

Bailey, N. and French, S. (2004: forthcoming) 'The 4 locational dynamics of financial services in regional cities', in N. Buck et al (eds) *City matters*, London: Palgrave.

Bank of England (2000) *Finance for small businesses in deprived communities*, London: Bank of England.

Bassett, K. (1996) 'Partnerships, business elites and urban politics: new forms of governance in an English city', *Urban Studies*, vol 33, no 3, pp 539-55.

Bassett, K., Griffiths, R. and Smith, I. (2002) 'Testing governance: partnerships, planning and conflict in waterfront regeneration', *Urban Studies*, vol 39, no 10, pp 1757-75.

BCC (Bristol City Council) (1998) *Bristol democracy plan*, Bristol: BCC.

BCC (2000) *Media: Bristol*, Bristol: BCC.

BDC (Bristol Democracy Commission) (2001) *Local democracy in Bristol*, Bristol: BDC.

Beddow, N. (2001) *Turning point*, Exeter: South West Arts.

Begg, I. (1999) 'Cities and competitiveness', *Urban Studies*, vol 36, nos 5-6, pp 795-80.

Begg, I. (2002) *Urban competitiveness: Policies for dynamic cities*, Bristol: The Policy Press.

Begg, I., Moore, B. and Altunbas, Y. (2001) *Economic change in cities: Influences on urban competitive advantage and prospects for the British urban system*, Final report of project for ESRC Cities and Competitiveness Programme, mimeo.

Begg, I., Moore, B. and Altunbas, Y. (2002) 'Long-run trends in the competitiveness of British cities', in I. Begg (ed) *Urban competitiveness: Policies for dynamic cities*, Bristol: The Policy Press, pp 101-34.

Berghman, J. (1995) 'Social exclusion in Europe: policy context and analytical framework', in G. Room (ed) *Beyond the threshold: The measurement and analysis of social exclusion*, Bristol: The Policy Press.

Bibby, P. and Shepherd, J. (1995) Urbanisation in England, London: HMSO.

Bibby, P. and Shepherd, J. (2001) 'Re-focusing brownfield housing targets, part 1: bringing in the settlement pattern', *Town and Country Planning*, vol 70, December, pp 327-31.

Boddy, M. (1999) 'Geographical economics and urban competitiveness: a critique', *Urban Studies*, vol 26, nos 5-6, pp 811-42.

Boddy, M. and Parkinson, M. (eds) (2004: forthcoming) *City matters: Competitveness, cohesion and urban governance*, Bristol: The Policy Press.

Boddy, M., Lovering, J. and Bassett, K. (1986) *Sunbelt city? A study of economic change in Britain's M4 growth corridor*, Oxford: Clarendon Press.

Boddy, M., Lambert, C., French, S. and Smith, I. (1999) *Bristol business survey: A survey of major employers*, Bristol: Joint Structure Plan and Transportation Unit.

Boyden Southwood Associates (1992) *A cultural strategy for Bristol*, Bristol: Boyden Southwood.

Bramley, G. (1999) 'The changing physical form of cities: trends, explanations and implications', Paper presented to ESRC UK/US workshop on Cities, Competitiveness and Cohesion, Glasgow, November.

Bramley, G. and Lambert, C. (2002) 'Managing urban development: land-use planning and city competitiveness', in I. Begg (ed) *Urban competitiveness: Policies for dynamic cities*, Bristol: The Policy Press, pp 283-310.

Breheny, M. (ed) (1999) *The people: Where will they work?*, London: Town and Country Planning Association.

Brennan, A., Rhodes, J. and Tyler, P. (2000) 'The nature of local area social exclusion in England and the role of the labour market', *Oxford Review of Economic Policy*, vol 16, no 1, pp 129-46.

Bristol 2000 (undated) *Our millennium vision*, Bristol: Bristol 2000.

Bristow, G., Gripaios, P. and Munday, M. (1999) 'Financial and business services and uneven economic development: some Welsh evidence', *Tijdschrift voor Economische en Sociale Geografie*, vol 90, no 2, pp 156-67.

Bristow, G., Munday, M. and Gripaios, P. (2000) 'Call centre growth and location: corporate strategy and the spatial division of labour', *Environment and Planning A*, vol 32, pp 519-38.

BRP (Bristol Regeneration Partnership) (2001) *Getting there: A regeneration framework for Bristol*, Bristol: BRP.

Buck, N. (2001) 'Identifying neighbourhood effects on social exclusion', *Urban Studies*, vol 38, no 12, pp 2251-75.

Burchardt, T., Le Grand, J. and Piachaud, D. (1999) 'Social exclusion in Britain, 1991-95', *Social Policy and Administration*, vol 33, no 3, pp 227-44.

Burton, D., Knights, D., Leyshon, A., Alferoff, C. and Signoretta, P. (2003) 'Making a market: the rise of the "sub-prime" market within the retail financial services industry', Mimeograph, available from A. Leyshon, School of Geography, University of Nottingham, Nottingham, NG7 2RD, UK (email: Andrew.Leyshon@Nottingham.ac.uk).

Butler, T. and G. Robson (2001) 'Social capital, gentrification and neighbourhood change in London: a comparison of three South London neighbourhoods', *Urban Studies*, vol 38, no 12, pp 2145-62.

Byrne, D. (2001) *Understanding the urban*, Basingstoke: Palgrave.

Cabinet Office (2000) *Reaching out: The role of central government at regional and local level*, Performance and Innovation Unit, Cabinet Office, London: The Stationery Office.

Cambridge Econometrics (2002) *Industry and the British economy*, Cambridge: Cambridge Econometrics.

CBI (Confederation of British Industry) (1988) *Initiatives beyond charity*, London: CBI.

CCG (Core Cities Group) (1999) *Core cities: Key centres for regeneration synthesis report*, Report prepared by D. Charles, D. Bradley, P. Chatterton, M. Coombes and A. Gillespie, Centre for Urban and Regional Development Studies, Newcastle: University of Newcastle.

Champion, A.G. (1999) 'Migration and British cities in the 1990s', *National Institute Economic Review*, no 170, pp 60-77.

Cheshire, P. and Magrini, S. (2002) 'Competitiveness in European cities – what can we learn?', Workshop on urban governance, economic competitiveness and social cohesion, Worcester College, 7-9 April, Oxford: (mimeo).

Clements, R. (1969) *Local notables and the city council*, London: Macmillan.

Collard, S., Kempson, E. and Whyley, C. (2001) *Tackling financial exclusion: An area-based approach*, Bristol: The Policy Press.

Collinge, C. and Srbjlanin, A. (2002) 'A network paradigm for urban governance?', in R. Hambleton, H. Savitch and M. Stewart (eds) *Globalism and local democracy*, Basingstoke: Palgrave.

Community at Heart (1999) *New Deal for Communities*, Delivery Plan, Bristol: Community at Heart.

Cooke, P., Davies, C. and Wilson, R. (2002) 'Urban networks and the new economy: the impact of clusters on planning for growth', in I. Begg (ed) *Urban competitiveness: Policies for dynamic cities*, Bristol: The Policy Press, pp 233-56.

Creative Industries Task Force (1998) *Creative Industries Mapping Document*, London: Department for Culture, Media and Sport.

Davies, G. (2000a) 'Narrating the Natural History Unit: institutional orderings and spatial strategies', *Geoforum*, vol 31, no 4, pp 539-51.

Davies, G. (2000b) 'Science, observation and entertainment: competing visions of post-war British natural history television', *Ecumene*, vol 7, no 4, pp 432-60.

De Groot, L. (1992) 'City challenge: competing in the urban regeneration game', *Local Economy*, vol 7, no 3.

Deas, I. and Giordano, B. (2002) 'Locating the competitive city in England', in I. Begg (ed) *Urban competitiveness: Policies for dynamic cities*, Bristol: The Policy Press, pp 191-210.

Deas, I. and Ward, K. (1999) 'From the new localism to the new regionalism: the implications of RDAs for city–regional relations', *Political Geography*, vol 19, no 3, pp 273-92.

DETR (Department of the Environment, Transport and the Regions) (1994) *Planning Policy Guidance Note 13 Transport (PPG13)*, London: The Stationery Office.

DETR (2000a) *Our towns and cities. The future: Delivering an urban renaissance*, Cm 4911, London: The Stationery Office.

DETR (2000b) *Planning Policy Guidance Note 3 Housing (PPG3)*, London: The Stationery Office.

DETR (2000c) *Indices of deprivation 2000*, Research Regeneration Summary Number 31, London: DETR.

DETR (2000d) *Modernising local government*, London: DETR.

DETR (2000e) 'Local action to counter exclusion: a research review', in *Joining it up locally: The evidence base*, Report of Policy Action Team 17, vol 2, London: DETR.

Dickens, R., Gregg, P. and Wadsworth, J. (2000) 'New Labour and the labour market', *Oxford Review of Political Economy*, no 16, pp 95-113.

DiGaetano, A. and Klemanski, J.S. (2000) *Power and city governance*, Minneapolis, MN/London: University of Minnesota.

Dresser, M. and Ollerenshaw, P. (1996) *The making of modern Bristol*, Bristol: Redcliffe Press.

DTI (Department of Trade and Industry) (2001) *Business clusters in the UK: A first assessment*, London: DTI.

DTLR (Department of Transport, Local Government and the Regions) (2001a) *Planning: Delivering a fundamental change*, London: DTLR.

DTLR (2001b) *Local strategic guidance: Accreditation*, London: DETR.

Eccles, R.G. and Crane, D.B. (1988) *Doing deals: Investment banks at work*, Boston, MA: Harvard Business School.

Featherstone, M. (1991) *Consumer culture and postmodernism*, London: Sage Publications.

Fielding, A.J. (1991) 'Migration and social mobility: south east England as an escalator region', *Regional Studies*, vol 26, no 1, pp 1-15.

Forrest, R. and Kearns, A. (2001) 'Social cohesion, social capital and the neighbourhood', *Urban Studies*, vol 38, no 12, pp 2125-43.

French, S. (2000) 'Rescaling the economic geography of knowledge and information: constructing life assurance markets', *Geoforum*, vol 31, pp 101-19.

French, S. (2002) 'Gamekeepers and gamekeeping: assuring Bristol's place within life underwriting', *Environment and Planning A*, vol 34, pp 513-41.

Gardener, E.P.M. and Molyneux, P. (1990) *Changes in Western European banking*, London: Unwin Human.

Garreau, J. (1991) *Edge city: Life on the new frontier*, New York, NY: Doubleday/Anchor.

Giddens, A. (1998) *The third way*, Cambridge: Polity Press.

Gillespie, A. (1999) 'The changing employment geography of Britain', in M. Breheny (ed) *The people: Where will they work?*, London: TCPA, pp 9-28.

Gordon, D., Adelman, A., Ashworth, K., Bradshaw, J., Levitas, R., Middleton, S., Pantazis, C., Patsios, D., Payne, S., Townsend, P. and Williams, J. (2000) *Poverty and social exclusion in Britain*, York: Joseph Rowntree Foundation (www.bris.ac.uk/poverty/pse/).

Grabher, G. (1993) 'The weakness of strong ties', in G. Grabher (ed) *The embedded firm: On the socioeconomics of industrial networks*, London: Routledge.

Green, A.E. and Owen, D.W. (1990) 'The development of a classification of travel to work areas', *Progress in Planning*, vol 34, no 1, pp 1-92.

Green A.E., Hogarth, T. and Shackleton, R.E. (1999) *Long distance living: Dual location households*, Bristol: The Policy Press.

Griffiths, R., Bassett, K. and Smith, I. (1999) 'Cultural policy and the cultural economy in Bristol', *Local Economy*, vol 14, no 3, pp 257-64.

Gripaios, P., Bristow, G. and Munday, M. (1999) 'Call centres' in the south west economy', *Trends & Prospects* (11th edn), Cambridge: Cambridge Econometrics, pp 35-7.

Guardian, The (2003) 'No jobs for the back room boys', R. Ramesh, 4 June.

Haldane, J.B.S. (1918) *Report of the machinery of government committee*, The Haldane Report, Cmnd 9230, London: HMSO.

Hall, P. (1995) 'Towards a general urban theory', in J. Brotchie, M. Batty, E. Blakely, P. Hall and P. Newton (eds) *Cities in competition: Productive and sustainable cities for the 21st century*, Melbourne: Longman, pp 3-31.

Hall, P. (1997) 'Modelling the post-industrial city', *Futures*, no 29, pp 311-22.

Hall, P., Thomas, H., Gracey, R. and Drewett, R. (1973) *The containment of urban England*, London: Geo Allen & Unwin.

Harding, A. (1994) 'Urban regimes and growth machines: towards a cross-national agenda', *Urban Affairs Quarterly*, vol 25, no 3, pp 285-98.

Hartshorn, T. and Muller, P.O. (1989) 'Suburban downtowns and the transformation: metropolitan Atlanta's business landscape', *Urban Geography*, no 10, pp 375-95.

Hastings, A. (1996) 'Unravelling the process of partnership in urban regeneration policy', *Urban Studies*, vol 33, no 2, pp 253-68.

Haughton, G. and Williams, C. (eds) (1996) *Corporate city*, Aldershot: Avebury.

Hills, J. (1998) *Income and wealth: The latest evidence*, York: Joseph Rowntree Foundation.

Hills, J. (1999) 'Social exclusion, income dynamics and public policy', Centre for the Analysis of Social Exclusion (CASE) Report 129, London: London School of Economics and Political Science.

HM Treasury (1999a) *Access to financial services: National strategy for neighbourhood renewal*, Report of Policy Action Team 14, London: HM Treasury.

HM Treasury (1999b) *Enterprise and social exclusion: National strategy for neighbourhood renewal*, Report of Policy Action Team 3, London: HM Treasury

Hobcraft, J. (1998) 'Intergenerational and life course transmission of social exclusion: influences of child poverty, family disruption and contact with the police', Centre for the Analysis of Social Exclusion (CASE) Paper 15, London: London School of Economics and Political Science.

Hobcraft, J. (2000) 'The roles of schooling and educational qualifications in the emergence of adult social exclusion', Centre for the Analysis of Social Exclusion (CASE) Paper 43, London: London School of Economics and Political Science.

Holliday, I. (2000) 'Is the British state hollowing out?', *Political Quarterly*, vol 71, no 2, pp 167-76.

Howarth, C., Kenway, P., Palmer, G. and Miorelli, R. (1999) *Monitoring poverty and social exclusion 1999*, York: Joseph Rowntree Foundation.

Huxham, C. (ed) (1996) *Creating collaborative advantage*, London: Sage Publications.

Huxham, C. and Vangen, S. (2000) 'Perspectives on leadership in collaboration: how things happen in a (not quite) joined up world', Working Paper 8, Faculty of the Built Environment, Bristol: UWE.

Jessop, B. (1995) 'The regulation approach: governance and post-Fordism: alternative perspectives', *Economy and Society*, vol 24, no 3, pp 307-33.

JRF (Joseph Rowntree Foundation) (1995) *Income and wealth: Report of the JRF inquiry group*, vols 1 and 2, York: Joseph Rowntree Foundation

JSPTU (Joint Structure Planning and Transportation Unit) (1998) *Replacement structure plan for the Avon area*, Bristol: JSPTU.

Kearns, A. and Forrest, R. (2000) 'Social cohesion and multi-level urban governance', *Urban Studies*, vol 37, nos 5-6, pp 995-1017.

Keith, M. and Pile, S. (1993) *Place and the politics of identity*, London: Routledge.

Kelly, A. and Kelly, M. (2000) *Impact and values: Assessing the arts and creative industries in the south west*, Bristol: Bristol Cultural Development Partnership.

Kimberlee, R., Hoggett, P. and Stewart, M. (2000) *The Bristol Regeneration Partnership's SRB4 Scheme: First interim evaluation*, Bristol: UWE.

Kleinman, M. (1998) 'Include me out? The new politics of place and poverty', Centre for the Analysis of Social Exclusion (CASE) Paper 11, London: London School of Economics and Political Science.

Kloosterman, R.C. and Musterd, S. (2001) 'The polycentric urban region: towards a research agenda', *Urban Studies*, vol 38, no 4, pp 623-33.

Krugman, P. (1994) *Peddling prosperity: Economic sense and nonsense in the age of diminished reason*, New York, NY: W.W. Norton Ltd.

Kumar, A. and Paddison, R. (2000) 'Trust and collaborative planning theory: the case of the Scottish planning system', *International Planning Studies*, vol 5, no 2, pp 205-33.

Lambert, C. and Boddy, M. (2002) 'Transforming the city: post-recession gentrification and re-urbanisation', Centre for Neighbourhood Research (CNR) Paper 6, Bristol: CNR (www.neighbourhoodcentre.org.uk).

Lambert, C. and Oatley, N. (2002), 'Governance, institutional capacity and planning for growth', in G. Cars, P. Healey, A. Madanipour and C. de Magalhaes (eds) *Urban governance, institutional capacity and social milieux*, Aldershot, Ashgate.

Lash, S. and Urry, J. (1994) *Economies of signs and space*, London: Sage Publications.

Lauria, M. (ed) (1997) *Reconstructing urban regime theory: Regulating urban politics in a global economy*, Thousand Oaks, CA: Sage Publications.

Lees, L. (2000) 'A reappraisal of gentrification: towards a "geography of gentrification"', *Progress in Human Geography*, vol 24, no 3, pp 389-408.

Lenoir, R. (1974) *Les exclus*, Paris: Seuil.

Levitas, R. (1996) 'The concept of social exclusion and the new Durkheimian hegemony', *Critical Social Policy*, no 46, pp 5-20.

Levitas, R. (1998) *The inclusive society? Social exclusion and New Labour*, London: Macmillan Press.

Leyshon, A. and Pollard, J. (2000) 'Geographies of industrial convergence: the case of retail banking', *Transactions of the Institute of British Geographers*, no 25, pp 203-20.

Leyshon, A. and Thrift, N. (1997) *Money/space: Geographies of monetary transformation*, London: Routledge.

Leyshon A. and Thrift, N. (1999) 'Lists come alive: electronic systmes of knowledge and the rise of credit scoring in banking', *Economy and Society*, vol 28, pp 434-66.

Leyshon, A., Thrift, N. and Tommey, C. (1989) 'The rise of the British provincial financial centre', *Progress in Planning*, no 31, pp 151-229.

Leyshon, A., Burton, D., Knights, D., Alferoff, C. and Signortetta, P. (2004: in press) 'Ecologies of retail financial services: understanding the persistence of door-to-door credit and insurance providers', *Environment and Planning A*.

Logan, J.R. and Molotch, H.L. (1987) *Urban fortunes: The political economy of space*, Berkeley, CA: University of California Press.

Lowe, M. (2000) 'Britain's regional shopping centres: new urban forms', *Urban Studies*, vol 37, no 2, pp 261-74.

McGuigan, J. (1996) *Culture and the public sphere*, London: Routledge.

Machin, S. (1998) 'Childhood disadvantage and intergenerational transmissions of economic status', in A. Atkinson, and J. Hills (eds) *Exclusion, employment and opportunity*, Centre for the Analysis of Social Exclusion (CASE) Paper 4, London, London School of Economics and Political Science, pp 56-64.

Mackintosh, M. (1993) 'Partnership: issues of policy and negotiation', *Local Economy*, vol 7, no 3.

Malpass, P. (1994) 'Policy making and local governance: how Bristol failed to secure City Challenge Funding (twice)', *Policy & Politics*, vol 22, no 4, pp 301-12.

Marsh, D. and Rhodes, R.A.W. (eds) (1992) *Policy networks in British government*, Oxford: Clarendon Press.

Miller, C. (1999) 'Partners in regeneration: constructing a local regime for urban management', *Policy & Politics*, vol 27, no 3, pp 343-58.

Miller, D.C. (1958a) 'Decision making cliques in community power structures: a comparative study of an American and an English city', *American Journal of Sociology*, vol 61, pp 299-310.

Miller, D.C. (1958b) 'Industry and community power structure: a comparative study of an American and an English city', *American Sociological Review*, vol 23, pp 9-15.

Oatley, N. and Lambert, C. (1995) 'Evaluating competitive urban policy: the City Challenge Initiative', in R. Hambleton and H.Thomas (eds) *Urban policy evaluation*, London: Paul Chapman Publishing.

ODPM (Office of the Deputy Prime Minister) (2003a) *Creating sustainable communities: Building for the future*, London: ODPM.

ODPM (2003b) *Planning Policy Guidance Note 3. Housing – influencing the size, type and affordability of housing*, London: ODPM.

Owen, C.J. (1994) 'City government in Plock: an emerging urban regime in Poland?', *Journal of Urban Affairs*, vol 16, no 1, pp 67-80.

Pacione, M. (1997) (ed) *Britain's cities*, London: Routledge.

Parr, J.B. and Budd, L. (2000) 'Financial services and the urban system: an exploration', *Urban Studies*, vol 37, no 3, pp 593-610.

Parsons, C. (1982) *True to nature*, Patrick Stephens Ltd.

Peck, J. and Tickell, A. (1995) 'Business goes local: dissecting the business agenda in Manchester', *International Journal of Urban and Regional Research*, vol 19, no 1, pp 55-78.

Punter, J. (1990) *Design control in Bristol 1940-1990*, Bristol: Redcliffe Press.

Purdue, D., Razzaque, K., Hambleton, R., Stewart, M. with Huxham, C. and Vangen, S. (2000) *Community leadership in area regeneration*, Bristol: The Policy Press.

Rhodes, R. (1994) 'The hollowing out of the state: the changing nature of public service in Britain', *Political Quarterly*, vol 65, pp 138-51.

Rhodes, R. (1997) *Understanding governance: Policy networks, governance, reflexivity and accountability*, Buckingham: Open University Press.

Richardson, R., Belt, V. and Marshall, N. (2000) 'Taking calls to Newcastle: the regional implications of the growth in call centres', *Regional Studies*, no 34, pp 357-69.

Robson, B., Peck, J. and Holden, A. (2000a) *Regional agencies and area-based regeneration*, Bristol: The Policy Press.

Robson, B., Parkinson, M., Boddy, M. and Maclennan, D. (2000b) *The state of English cities*, London: DETR.

RPG10 (2001) *Regional planning guidance for the south west*, London: DTLR.

Scott, A. (2000) *The cultural economy of cities*, London: Sage Publications.

Selwood S. (ed) (2001) *The UK cultural sector: Profile and policy issues*, London: Policy Studies Institute.

SEU (Social Exclusion Unit) (1998) *Bringing Britain together: A national strategy for neighbourhood renewal*, London: Cabinet Office.

SEU (2001) *A new commitment to neighbourhood renewal: National Strategy Action Plan*, London: Cabinet Office.

Sheffield City Council (1997) *Sheffield trends: An annual compilation of indicators for Sheffield*, Statistical Supplement, Sheffield: Sheffield City Council.

Simmie, J.M. (2002) 'Knowledge spillovers and the reasons for the concentration of innovative SMEs', *Urban Studies*, May.

Skelcher, C. and Lowndes, M. (1998) 'The dynamics of multi-organisational partnerships: an analysis of changing modes of governance', *Public Administration*, vol 76, no 2, pp 313-33.

Skelcher, C., Lowndes, M. and McCabe, A. (1996) *Community networks in urban regeneration: 'It all depends who you know'*, York: Joseph Rowntree Foundation.

Snape, D. and Stewart, M. (1996) 'Keeping up the momentum: partnership working in Bristol and the West of England', Report to the Bristol Chamber of Commerce and Initiative, Bristol: UWE.

Soja, E. (2000) *Postmetropolis: Critical studies of cities and regions*, Oxford: Blackwell.

South Gloucestershire Council (2000) *Local plan, deposit draft*, South Gloucestershire: South Gloucestershire Council.

Sparkes, J. (1999) 'Schools, education and social exclusion', Centre for the Analysis of Social Exclusion (CASE) Paper 29, London: London School of Economics and Political Science.

Stewart, M. (1976) 'Talking to local business: the involvement of Chambers of Commerce in local affairs', Working Paper 38, Bristol: SAUS Publications.

Stewart, M. (1986) 'Urban policy in Thatcher's England', Working Paper 90, Bristol: SAUS Publications.

Stewart, M. (1996) 'The politics of local complacency', *Journal of Urban Affairs*, vol 18, no 2.

Stewart, M. (1997) 'Participatory policy making: between divergence and convergence: a commentary', *European Journal of Work and Organisational Psychology*, vol 6, no 2, pp 219-25.

Stewart, M. (1998) 'Janus leadership', Working paper 20, Bristol: UWE.

Stewart, M. (2000) 'The politics of interdependence', in B. Blanke and R. Smith (eds) *Cities in transition: New challenges, new responsibilities*, London: Macmillan.

Stewart, M. (2002) 'Compliance and collaboration in urban governance', in P. Healey, G. Cars and A. Madanipour (eds) *Urban governance, institutional capacity and social milieux*, Aldershot: Ashgate.

Stewart, M., Goss, S., Clarke, R., Gillanders, G., Rowe, J. and Shaftoe, H. (1999) *Cross-cutting issues affecting local government*, London: DETR.

Stoker, G. and Mossberger, K. (1994) 'Urban regime theory in comparative perspective', *Environment and Planning C, Government and Policy*, vol 12, no 2, pp 195-212.

Storper, M. (1995) 'The resurgence of regional economies, ten years later: the region as a nexus of untraded interdependencies', *European Urban and Regional Studies*, vol 2, pp 191-221.

Sudjec, D. (1992) *The 100 mile city*, Orlando, FL: Harcourt Brace.

Sullivan, H. and Skelcher, C. (eds) (1992) *Working across boundaries: Collaboration in public services*, Basingstoke: Palgrave.

Sunday Times, The (2003) 'The great Indian takeaway', D. O'Connell and L. Armitstead, 8 June, Business Focus, p 5.

Sweeting, D. and Stewart, M. (1999) 'Towards future urban strategies: leadership in urban governance leadership', Working Paper 11, Faculty of the Built Environment, Bristol: UWE.

Taylor, A. (2000) 'Hollowing out or filling in? Taskforces and the management of cross-cutting issues in British government', *British Journal of Politics and International Relations*, vol 2, no 1, pp 46-71.

TBI (The Bristol Initiative) (1989) *Bristol: The challenge of the 1990s*, Bristol: The Bristol Initiative.

Thrift, N. (1994) 'On the social and cultural determinants of international financial centres: the case of the City of London', in S. Corbridge, R. Martin and N. Thrift (eds) *Money, power and space*, Oxford: Blackwell.

Turok, I. and Edge, N. (1999) *The jobs gap in Britain's cities: Employment loss and labour market consequences*, Bristol: The Policy Press.

Urban Task Force (1999) *Towards an urban renaissance*, London: E&FN Spon.

Valler, D. (1995) 'Local economic strategy and local coalition building', *Local Economy*, no 10, pp 33-48.

Webb, A. (1991) 'Co-ordination: a problem in public sector management', *Policy & Politics*, vol 19, no 4, pp 229-41.

Wenban-Smith, A. (2002) 'Sustainable institutional capacity for planning: the west Midlands', in G. Cars, P. Healey, A. Madanipour and C. de Magalhaes (eds) *Urban governance, institutional capacity and social milieux*, Aldershot: Ashgate.

Woolcock, M. (1998) 'Social capital and economic development: towards a theoretical synthesis and policy framework', *Theory and Society*, no 21, pp 151-208.

Zukin, S. (1995) *The cultures of cities*, Oxford: Blackwell.

Also available from The Policy Press

Urban competitiveness
Policies for dynamic cities
Edited by Ian Begg

The question of what makes some cities more successful than others has become an increasingly important policy issue. This topical book is the first to explore facets of competitiveness in a systematic way that combines theory, evidence and policy implications. Bringing together leading experts on urban economic performance, it provides a new look at the issue of urban competitiveness.

Paperback £19.99 ISBN 1 86134 357 4
Hardback £50.00 ISBN 1 86134 358 2
216 x 148mm 352 pages February 2002

Urban renaissance?
New Labour, community and urban policy
Edited by Rob Imre and Mike Raco

This book documents and assesses the core of New Labour's approach to the revitalisation of cities, that is, the revival of citizenship, democratic renewal, and the participation of communities to spear head urban change. In doing so, the book explores the meaning, and relevance, of 'community' as a focus for urban renaissance. It interrogates the conceptual and ideological content of New Labour's conceptions of community and, through the use of case studies, evaluates how far, and with what effects, such conceptions are shaping contemporary urban policy and practice.

Paperback £19.99 ISBN 1 86134 380 9
Hardback £50.00 ISBN 1 86134 381 7
234 x 156mm 304 pages May 2003

City matters
Competitiveness, cohesion and urban governance
Edited by Martin Boddy and Michael Parkinson

This book provides, in a single volume, a review of the findings of the largest ever programme of cities research in the UK, the Economic and Social Research Council's **'Cities: Competitiveness and Cohesion programme'**. Leading experts present the findings of this wide-ranging programme organised around themes of competitiveness, social cohesion and the role of policy and governance.

Paperback £25.00 ISBN 1 86134 444 9
Hardback £55.00 ISBN 1 86134 445 7
234 x 156mm 464 pages May 2004

To order further copies of this publication or any other Policy Press titles please contact:

In the UK and Europe:
Marston Book Services, PO Box 269,
Abingdon, Oxon, OX14 4YN, UK
Tel: +44 (0)1235 465500
Fax: +44 (0)1235 465556
Email: direct.orders@marston.co.uk

In the USA and Canada:
ISBS, 920 NE 58th Street, Suite 300,
Portland, OR, 97213-3786, USA
Tel: +1 800 944 6190 (toll free)
Fax: +1 503 280 8832
Email: info@isbs.com

In Australia and New Zealand:
DA Information Services, 648 Whitehorse
Road Mitcham, Victoria 3132, Australia
Tel: +61 (3) 9210 7777
Fax: +61 (3) 9210 7788
E-mail: service@dadirect.com.au

Further information about all of our titles can be found on our website:

www.policypress.org.uk